TOYS TO GROW WITH
Infants & Toddlers

TOYS TO

JOHN J. FISHER

Cocreator, Johnson & Johnson Child Development Toys

Photographs by Bill Parsons

Courtesy of Johnson & Johnson Child Development Toys

Illustrations by Jeffrey Dinardo

GROW WITH

Infants & Toddlers
Endless Play Ideas That Make Learning Fun

Developed by The Philip Lief Group, Inc.
A PERIGEE BOOK

Perigee Books
are published by
The Putnam Publishing Group
200 Madison Avenue
New York, NY 10016

Developed by The Philip Lief Group, Inc.,
319 East 52nd Street, New York, NY 10022
Published simultaneously in Canada by
General Publishing Co. Limited, Toronto

Photographs courtesy of Johnson & Johnson Child Development Products

Library of Congress Cataloging-in-Publication Data

Fisher, John J.
   Toys to grow with, infants & toddlers.

   "A Perigee book."
   1. Toys.   2. Play.   3. Child development.
I. Philip Lief Group.   II. Title.
HQ784.T68F57   1986   649'.55   85-30110
ISBN 0-399-51243-8

Book designed by The Sarabande Press

Printed in the United States of America
1   2   3   4   5   6   7   8   9   10

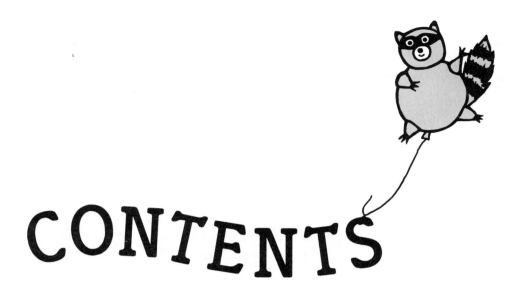

CONTENTS

HOMEMADE TOYS:
By Ideal Introduction Age

Ideal Intro Age	Age Range (Mos)	Toy
Birth	B–3	**EYE TARGETS** Colorful patterned discs to hang from the cribside.
Birth	B–3	**SHADOWBOX PICTURES** Dazzling watchables from gift boxes and wrapping paper.
Birth	B–3	**PICTURE PARADE** Stand-alone pictures for crib, carriage, changing table.
Birth	B–12	**CHANGING TABLE DISPLAY** Create a changeable display for diapering time.
6 Wks	6W–6M	**CHANGING-TIME MOBILE** Special watchables just for the changing table.
2 Mos	2–4	**BAT-A-BAG** Clever batting toy for the baby carriage.

2 Mos	2–18	**EXERCISE PORTA-PAD** Padded, washable, portable exercise and changing pad.
3 Mos	3–6	**PLAY BOX** A complete play gym for an infant seat.
3 Mos	3–12	**PICTURE LINE** Turns the nursery wall into an art gallery.
4 Mos	3–9	**GRABBABLE GLOVE** A super simple toy for reaching, grasping, exploring.
4 Mos	4–8	**SUPER KICKER** Soundmaking kicking toy to strengthen baby's legs.
6 Mos	4–12	**TRIPLE MITTENS** Plenty of handles for grasping and chewing on.
6 Mos	6–12	**TALKING SOCK** Squeezable, shakable, multi-sound manipulative.
6 Mos	6–12	**TOUCHABLE GLOVE** Texture glove that *you* wear—and your baby explores.
6 Mos	6–18	**BOXED PICTURES** Three-dimensional "book" perfect for the youngest readers.
6 Mos	6–36	**HUGGABLE BUTTERFLY** This simple-to-make stuffed toy is a great cuddly.
9 Mos	9–36	**TEXTURE CARDS** Give your baby many textures to explore at one sitting.
9 Mos	9–36	**T-SHIRT PILLOWS** Make all sizes—from ordinary T-shirts.
9 Mos	9–36	**SAND & SEA PLAYGROUND** All-in-one wading pool and sandbox (with cover).
10 Mos	10–24	**FUZZY CRAWL-THROUGH** Turn a carpet remnant into a textured crawling tunnel.
10 Mos	10–18	**INDOOR OBSTACLE COURSE** A special challenge for your crawler.

12 Mos	12–18	CLIMB & SLIDE A cushion and cardboard climbing/sliding board.
12 Mos	12–36	SOCK BEANBAGS Super simple and effective handling/tossing toys.
12 Mos	12–36	TEXTURE BOOK More textures—this time in a turn-the-page book.
12 Mos	12–36	GREAT BOOKS! Suggestions for personalized toddler books.
12 Mos	12–36	INFLATABLE TUB BOAT Water ring and plastic tub become a versatile water toy.
12 Mos	12–36	WALL-LINE SCRAPBOOK Original way to help your toddler learn about herself.
15 Mos	15–30	CONTAINER BANK A challenging Fill & Dump for challengeable toddlers.
15 Mos	15–36	PEEKING HOUSE A scaled-up twist on an old favorite game.
15 Mos	12–36	RAMPS FOR ROLLER GAMES Add new dimensions to any rolling toy.
15 Mos	15–36	BALANCE BRIDGE Toddler-sized balance beam; great for fantasy play, too.
15 Mos	15–36	BAND INSTRUMENTS All kinds of soundmakers for a home parade.
18 Mos	18–36	POSTING CARDS Even more challenging fill & dump for older toddlers.
18 Mos	15–36	POSTAL BOX BLOCKS Giant (and cheap) blocks for climbing and building play.
18 Mos	15–36	GROCERY BAG BLOCKS Giant (and free) paper blocks for building, tumbling on.
18 Mos	15–36	TODDLER TRAMPOLINE Fabric-covered floor exercise bouncer.

18 Mos	18–36	PUNCHING BAG Give your toddler's arms a real workout.
18 Mos	18–36	SURPRISE PICTURE BOARD This open-the-flap picture game helps build vocabulary.
24 Mos	24–36	PEOPLE PUZZLES Favorite first puzzles—they can even star your toddler.
24 Mos	24–36	COOKIE-CUTTER PUZZLE Shape-matching puzzle made from holiday objects.
24 Mos	24–36	SURPRISE TOUCH BOX What's in the box? A guessing game based on touch.
24 Mos	24–36	PLAY DOUGH Homemade clay for squishing, rolling, pounding.
24 Mos	24–36	BALLPOINT PAINT PEN Change an empty deodorant bottle into a painting pen.
24 Mos	24–36	TARGET TOSS A target-tossing game for eye-hand coordination.
24 Mos	24–36	HAND PADDLES Turn paper plates into paddles for "racquet" games.
24 Mos	18–36	SLIPPERY SLIDER Set up this outdoor water slide on sultry days.
24 Mos	24–36	MY BODY POSTER A poster room decoration for learning about the body.
24 Mos	24–36	BLUE JEANS BAG This fantasy bag also builds dressing skills.
24 Mos	24–36	ROAD RAMP 'N TUNNEL Add dimension to play with toy cars and trucks.
24 Mos	18–36	BOX CAR A nonmoving vehicle to inspire your young driver.

READ THIS FIRST

The more that child development specialists study the early years, the more they value young children's experiences, experiences that we can call play. Play is how a young child practices—and consequently perfects—emerging physical, mental, social, and language skills. Since development and learning are cumulative, early experiences are the foundation of nearly all future skills.

This isn't news to today's parents and teachers. You *know* that play is as important as it is fun. Yet, with so many responsibilities, so much to think about when raising a young child, it's not easy to be a play wizard, whether this is your first baby or your newest. As a mother exclaimed, "I know *why* play is so valuable. I need ideas of *what* to do!"

This book is filled with ideas:

○ What commercial and homemade toys are good for each age— and how to use them to enjoy and enhance all areas of your child's emerging skills.

○ 11 ○

o What games other parents (and experts) have found especially valuable at each developmental stage.

o What to do when you've exhausted your own bank of favorite play ideas or are just too exhausted to conjure up amazing new delights for your youngest family member.

And yes, there are illuminating discussions of *why* certain activities are so beneficial, too.

These play ideas and homemade toys come from years of research, both in libraries and in all kinds of daily environments: child care centers, special play labs, and most importantly homes. As cocreator of the Johnson & Johnson Child Development Toys, I've been lucky to work closely with hundreds of families and scores of teachers. I hope this book helps you enjoy your child's first three years, and makes learning through play even more fun for the whole family.

DO BABIES NEED TOYS?

Let's face it right up front: **Do babies need toys?**

Yes.

Throughout the early years your child develops all kinds of skills, from

hit-or-miss batting to reaching with sure coordination to understanding spatial relationships. Objects play a vital part.

For instance, consider physical skills, like reaching and grasping, using both hands simultaneously, or throwing with accuracy. To master these and scores of other skills, a baby needs to practice them over and over. Obviously, he needs objects with which to practice, objects that are safe and easy for him to handle.

Toys build intellectual skills, too. Young children learn best through direct experiences with the world around them. In a sense, they figure things out with their hands before their heads—and the former leads directly to the latter. By handling toys, stacking them into towers, knocking them down, fitting one toy over or into another, hiding and finding them, lining them up, counting them—in short, experimenting with all the ways parts can be related to one another—a young child learns concepts like size, shape, space, number, and the conservation of matter. According to Jean Piaget (one of the most influential and important child development experts):

> To think . . . is to classify, to arrange, to place in correspondence, to collect, to dissociate, etc. But all these operations must be carried out materially, in actions, in order to be capable afterward of being constructed in thought.

Toys can enhance language, social, and emotional skills as well, as you'll see throughout this book. Yes, babies do need toys.

But Remember . . .
This book considers a toy to be *any* object that your child plays with:

o Playthings you purchase (there are some excellent ones on the market).

o Toys you make at home (there are plenty of those in this book).

o Household objects culled from the kitchen, the scrapbox, the throw away pile.

And remember, too, toys are most successful when matched to your child's particular age or developmental stage. Toys that are too sophisticated will baffle or frustrate him (or, even worse, be dangerous); those that are too simple will bore. Your baby's play needs change as his interests and skills develop. So you need to decide when to introduce appropriate toys and games. There are guidelines throughout this book.

MAKING YOUR OWN TOYS

Among the scores of play ideas in this book are fifty toys you can make. Every one meets some very basic standards:

o All help your young child develop important skills.

o All have been tested with parents and children.

o All are made from common or easily obtained materials. In fact, most of these playthings can be made from a handful or two of indispensable items described in Homemade Toys: Invaluable Materials, page 189.

o Each serves a primary purpose that is not duplicated by a toy that you can buy. On the other hand, there are several well-designed commercial toys that are safer and more durable than anything you could hope to create without sophisticated machines and materials. Both serve an important purpose in your child's development.

o Since parents and teachers are so busy, all are simple to create. In fact, *each toy can be made in about thirty minutes—or less.*

SAFETY ESSENTIALS

Most toys made by reputable United States companies conform to safety codes. This has helped reduce toy-related accidents—provided that the toy is used by a child of the appropriate age (which doesn't always happen). Naturally, though, toys you make can't be covered by these manufacturing standards. Then again, many homemade toys and household items are wonderful for supervised play, but might become dangerous should a child use them without your watchful eye. All the homemade toys included here have been devised with safety in mind. Please heed the warning if a toy is indicated FOR SUPERVISED PLAY ONLY. You'll also find all kinds of SAFETY NOTES throughout this book, some general, some related to specific playthings (commercial as well as homemade). It's a good idea to read them.

A NOTE ON ORGANIZATION

These games and toys are organized into general skill areas: Early Eye-Catchers (visual stimulation for a very young baby), Activities for Hands (and Heads), Active Play & Exercise, and the like. Some categories are subdivided, too, where appropriate. Keep in mind that such divisions are arbitrary and by no means restrictive. Almost every toy, every game, enhances more than a single skill, no matter how broad the category.

The toys and games within a category (and sometimes subcategory) are generally listed chronologically by the child's age. Nearly all suggest the appropriate introductory age as well. This is also somewhat arbitrary—every baby is different, grows and learns at his own rate, and has an individual pattern of development.

And lastly, each homemade toy has specific age guidelines.

○ The *ideal intro age* is the age at which most children begin using the toy for its primary purpose—be it batting or handling or climbing or fantasy play.

○ The *age range* is the total stretch of time most children will enjoy the toy.

Sometimes the age range begins before the ideal age of introduction. For example, although many children enjoy some facets of the Toddler Trampoline starting at 15 months (or even younger), it's at 18 months that this toy really comes into its own.

These age guidelines are based mostly on children's typical behavior,   ○ 15 ○

sometimes on safety considerations. To repeat, *they are only guidelines.* Since your child is unique, he may enjoy an activity before or after the age given. You know your child best. Adapt the ages as you see fit.

NOTE: For a quick reference to all the homemade toys by *ideal intro age* and *age range,* see the table on pages 7–10.

NOTES AND REMINDERS

1. If you have older children as well as a baby or toddler, invite them to join in activities when appropriate. They might help you make some of these toys, too. Seeing (and helping) their younger sibling enjoy a toy they have created can alleviate a lot of jealous feelings.

2. Gather a friend or few for a toy-making session, like traditional barn raisings and quilting bees. And trade off projects. You might be a stitching wizard, your friend a graphics genius.

    NOTE: For a quick reference on which toys require which skills and materials, see Homemade Toys: By Materials and Techniques, page 192.

3. So much of how your child enjoys a particular game or toy depends on your own enthusiasm. The buoyant parent truly *can* make a silk purse out of a sow's ear.

4. Not every young child will be crazy about every game or toy in this book. After all, each of us has personal preferences. That's one reason why I've included so many ideas. (I certainly don't expect anyone to play all these games!) Try anything that strikes your fancy, but don't force it if your child is unenthusiastic. And if he snubs that dazzling toy you've made today, offer it at a future date. Or pass it along to another child.

5. He? She? Which pronoun to use? The familiar complaint. Yet there still is no genderless reference. Since children do come in two sexes, half these chapters call the child "he," the other half "she."

EARLY EYE-CATCHERS

VISUAL PLAY FOR THE FIRST MONTHS

Most experts who study newborns agree that a baby is eager to learn and play right from birth. But with limited physical skills, she isn't able to explore actively. She cannot yet control her arm and hand movements, for instance, so she's unable to reach for and handle objects skillfully. Nor can she crawl or walk to get those things that interest her. In a wry way, she embodies (and reinterprets) the old quotation: "The spirit is willing but the flesh is weak." Therefore, a tiny baby explores her new world most actively with her eyes.

Much early play is visual. In fact, even in the delivery room a baby will stare at faces or a picture of a face, and will follow such a picture when it is moved slowly past her eyes. In addition, researchers have found that babies like to look at simple shapes and patterns that contrast sharply against a background color. A black and white checkerboard, a distinct face on a stuffed toy, or even a simple brilliant red circle on a light-colored field catches their eye.

Even though babies can see from birth, their vision isn't perfect. Based on numerous studies, it's believed that newborns focus best on objects about eight to twelve inches from their eyes. Those closer or further away, though still visible, are blurred. Since your very young baby isn't able to bring things within her range of vision by herself, she depends on you to perk up her immediate surroundings.

HOMEMADE VISUAL DELIGHTS

One way to make your baby's world more exciting is to place bright, simple pictures wherever she may be: cradle or crib, carriage, or changing table.

Keep in mind that even very young babies like variety, so make several visual delights, and change them often.

Homemade Eye-Targets entertain your baby from the earliest weeks.

HINT: Looking at an eye-catcher, especially a face, can sometimes even calm a fussy baby, unless she's hungry or physically uncomfortable.

EYE TARGETS

Colorful patterned discs to hang from the cribside.
Ideal Intro Age: Birth
Age Range: Birth to 3 Months

Tools & Materials

○ Uncoated white paper plates

○ Felt-tipped markers; use nontoxic ones, just in case your baby should ever chew on these toys

○ Thick yarn or ribbon

○ Single hole punch or scissors

Directions

1. Draw a bold, simple design on each side of each plate. Good ideas include:

   ○ A bull's-eye

   ○ Checks

   ○ Giant polka dots

   ○ Broad stripes

   ○ Stars

   ○ Simple flowers

   ○ Faces; these are by far the favorites, so make several

2. Punch a hole in the top of each plate and hang it on the side of the crib or carriage with a short piece of yarn. The bottom of the plate should just about touch the mattress.

HINT: You can buy decorated plates at card shops and stationery stores that sell party supplies. Choose simple patterns.

SAFETY NOTE: Remove any paper toys from the crib or carriage when your baby begins reaching for them—usually between 2 and 3 months. The paper is unsafe for her to chew on.

SHADOWBOX PICTURES

Chances are your baby receives presents of clothing that come in small, flat boxes. Use these and the paper they're wrapped in to make dazzling watchables.
Ideal Intro Age: Birth
Age Range: Birth to 3 months

Tools & Materials

- Small, shallow gift box

- Wrapping paper with bold patterns

- Cellophane tape

- Thick yarn or ribbon

- Hole punch or scissors

Directions

1. Wrap the box top in paper. (To make two Shadow-box Pictures, wrap the bottom, separately, as well.) Completely cover the face and four narrow sides, securing the ends of the paper on the underside.

2. Punch a hole in one long, narrow side. Thread a short piece of yarn or ribbon through the hole, making a strong knot on the inside end, and hang in the crib or carriage as shown. The toy's bottom should just about touch the crib mattress.

SAFETY NOTE: Remove any paper toys from the crib when your baby begins reaching for them—usually between 2 and 3 months. The paper is unsafe for her to chew on.

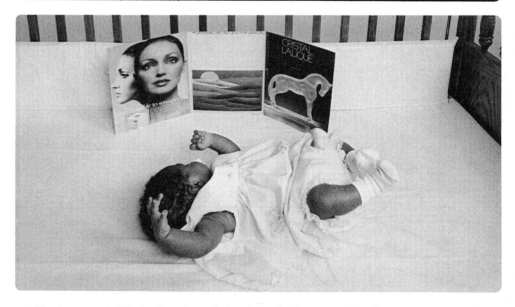

The homemade Picture Parade perks up the crib, changing table, floor—wherever baby plays.

PICTURE PARADE

Stand-alone pictures for crib, carriage, changing table, or play-pen (if you start using one early). This is also a terrific accordion book for the older baby.
Ideal Intro Age: Birth
Age Range: Birth to 3 Months (when baby plays alone)
Birth to 12 Months (in supervised play)

Tools & Materials

○ 3 sheets of cardboard, all the same size (about 8″ × 10″, although the actual dimensions aren't critical)

○ Old magazines with plenty of full-page color photographs or advertisements

○ White glue

○ Cellophane tape, at least 1″ wide

○ Clear Con-Tact paper (self-stick plastic film) (optional)

○ Scissors

Directions

1. Cut out six large pictures the same size as the cardboard sheets. Glue a picture to each side of each sheet.
    HINT: Let your baby help you choose the pictures to include. Look through magazines together, and use those things that really catch her eye.

2. Lay the sheets side by side, about an eighth of an inch apart. This gap will become a hinge that lets you fold up the finished toy. Tape the sheets together to make a panel of three pictures.

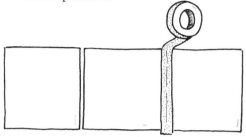

3. Turn the panel over and run a second piece of tape over each gap to complete the hinge.
4. For added durability, completely cover each side with clear Con-Tact paper.

SAFETY NOTE: This toy could be dangerous for the unsupervised baby over three months. She might gum or chew off a corner and choke on it.

PLAY TIPS

Your baby will also like looking at these homemade eye toys when lying on your lap or any flat surface, or, even later, when sitting in her infant seat. (Obviously, you'll have to hold them up for her to see.)

Talk about the pictured objects she's looking at—their colors and shapes, the parts of faces and their happy expressions, the stars just like those in the sky at night—whatever you can think of to describe them. Your baby won't understand all these words, naturally, but she loves listening to your voice. Over time she'll pick up on what she's hearing.

All these toys for the eyes take on added interest if they move. With your baby lying on her back, s-l-o-w-l-y move a watchable back and forth in front of her eyes. She probably *tracks* its movement (follows the toy with her eyes, as if she's watching a tiny tennis match). From about 2 months or so, she moves her head as well to keep the toy in view.

You can play tracking games with any toy that has bright colors and eye-catching patterns. Or put on a nice, bright glove and move your hand for her to track (wiggle your fingers, too). Or let her track your face.

CHANGING TIME WATCHABLES

Parents often ask me: "What can I do to keep my baby happily occupied on the changing table?" I'm not sure whether this question is prompted because they seek new play opportunities, or because they need to keep their baby busy so they can get along with the business at hand. Either way, here are some homemade toy ideas that fill the bill:

○ Changing Table Display

○ Changing-time Mobile

HINT: The homemade Picture Parade is dandy for the changing table, too.

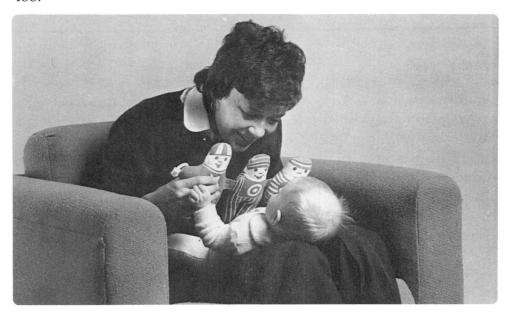

SAFETY NOTE: *Never* leave your baby alone on the changing table, no matter how young she may be. In the moment you're gone to answer the door or take a phone call, she might wriggle off.

CHANGING TABLE DISPLAY

A changeable display for diapering time.
Ideal Intro Age: Birth
Age Range: Birth to 12 Months

Tools & Materials

- Accordion-type wall rack, with several protruding pegs

- Eye-appealing toys: Eye Targets, Shadowbox Pictures, brightly decorated small shopping bags (folded flat), small stuffed animal, rattle, etc.

Directions

Mount the rack on the wall next to the changing table, and hang eye toys from the hooks.

HINT: Since your young baby focuses best on objects about eight to twelve inches away, put the changing table near or against the wall. When she begins reaching for the hanging objects—at around 3 months, when, coincidentally, she can focus on things up to a few feet distant—move the table away from the wall.

CHANGING-TIME MOBILE

This special mobile is good once your baby starts looking up, rather than off to the side, when lying on her back (usually around 6 weeks). The arms swing horizontally so you can position toys right where your baby is looking at the moment.

Ideal Intro Age: 6 Weeks

Age Range: 6 Weeks to 6 Months

Tools & Materials

- Fold-away towel rack with three arms

- Objects to catch the baby's eye:

  - Fancy bows from gift boxes

  - Small toys

  - Small Eye Targets (decorated dessert-sized paper plates; punch a hole through the center of each plate and hang them so they face down toward your baby)

  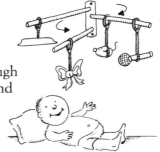

  - Small disposable aluminum pie plates, suspended like the Eye Targets

Directions

Mount the rack on the wall beside the changing table. Make sure it's high enough above the table surface (at least 30 inches) so that it won't interfere with changing—now, or later when your baby is more active. Use pieces of thick yarn or ribbon to hang the visual toys from the arms. Remember: for the early months, it's best if the toys hang about 12 inches from her eyes. However, if she can reach up and grab them at this distance, raise them slightly. These are objects to look at, not handle.

HINT: When your baby *can* grab objects dangling above her (usually starting around 3 or 4 months), replace these watchables with grabbables: rattles, squeak toys, favorite hand toys, and the like. Hang them from elastic straps, so that when your baby tugs them she doesn't loosen the rack from the wall.

CRIB MOBILES

Nearly everyone buys a crib mobile, the most traditional eye-catcher for the early months. In fact, a recent survey reported that over 90 percent of American babies had one. This statistic has not passed the toy industry by, and many mobiles available today (unlike those a few years ago) are well designed.

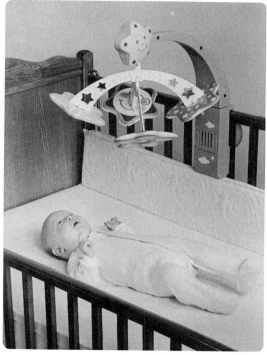

The appeal of the best mobiles is simple: the eye-catching visual toys rotate slowly while music plays. Since you'd be hard-pressed to make one that functions as well, consider buying one. And look for the following features:

○ Music. Your baby will enjoy this feature right from birth. In fact, the appealing tinkly music-box sound will soothe her during

A crib mobile is almost a given; check out the guidelines in this chapter for choosing a good one.

mildly fussy bouts. The visuals will be less important until she tends to look up rather than off to the side when lying on her back—usually starting around 6 weeks.

o The music box should play ten minutes or longer on a single winding. Otherwise you'll need to wind it frequently, and the cratchety sound this makes is *not* music to your baby's ears.

o Visuals should face downward, toward baby. If you can reverse them—added interest!—so much the better.

o The support arm should swing sideways, out of the way; this makes it easier to change the crib sheets.

o AS A BONUS: if the mobile can also be mounted on the wall, then you can use it (perhaps beside the changing table) when it outlives its usefulness in the crib.

SAFETY NOTE: You should probably remove a mobile from the crib when your baby can sit or pull herself to standing, usually between 5 and 6 months. Otherwise she'll probably rip it down—and most mobiles are *not* safe for a baby to handle.

HINT: Once you've removed the mobile, hang a colorful kite on the ceiling. It'll catch baby's eye and will move delightfully in a breeze. Make sure you attach it securely to a hook or other anchor in the ceiling—it might be dangerous if it fell into the crib.

SEEING GAMES FOR LATER MONTHS

Even though your baby starts life nearsighted, she develops normal eyesight in a fairly short time. By about 2 or 3 months, she can focus on objects anywhere from a few inches to several feet away. And by about 6 months, a baby can see as well as an adult with normal 20/20 vision. Whatever her age, though, she'll continue to enjoy eye games—such as these:

From about 2 months: When she's lying on her back, let her track a toy all the way from one side of her head to the other.

From about 2 months, your baby likes to follow toys that move slowly past her face.

From about 3 months: Lay your baby on her stomach. Dangle a toy in front of her face, then raise it slowly into the air. As she pushes up on her arms to keep the toy in view, she exercises arm and back muscles, too.

From about 4 to 6 months on: You know how popular special effects are in movies. Create some for your baby:

- Let her watch you blow soap bubbles.

- Hang a prism in the nursery window. On sunny days it will make rainbows on the wall.

- Wiggle your fingers in front of a flashlight to make shadow pictures on the wall of the darkened nursery. Or use the flashlight to pick out different objects in the room, such as pictures on the wall.

- On a sunny day, sit together beneath a window. Make shadow pictures on the floor.

Soap bubbles catch the older baby's eye.

TO SUM UP

Even though eyes are probably your very young baby's best tools for exploring and playing, she's ready for lots of other activities as well. In the next chapter you'll find toys and things for busy hands (and heads). ○ 29 ○

ACTIVITIES FOR HANDS (AND HEADS)

Most psychologists call the first eighteen or so months of life the *sensorimotor period.* This is the time your young child actively explores objects with his five senses: sight, hearing, smell, taste, and touch. And does he explore! One researcher, Allison Clarke-Stewart, found that the 9- to 18-month-olds she observed in their homes spent nearly 50 percent of their waking hours looking at and playing with objects.

How about the remaining time? About 36 percent was spent interacting with a parent, 18 percent having physical needs satisfied—i.e., feeding, dressing, bathing, and so forth. Some time, too, was spent just practicing large muscle skills, like pulling to stand and walking. As you might expect, there was some overlap from category to category; for instance, when a mother and child played together with a toy, this counted both as the child's playing with objects and as the child's interacting with a parent.

All this exploring leads to learning—about the physical properties of things, about how objects work and can be related to other objects— really, about how the world works. Remember that young children learn by *doing,* and the younger the child, the more this is true. While your child explores he learns about himself, too—what he can and can't do, what he likes and dislikes. He also practices an enormous range of physical skills (also called motor skills). Hence the name: *sensorimotor.*

Most of the games in this book develop sensorimotor skills—and, not incidentally, mental ones in the bargain. This chapter looks at activities primarily for the hands (and head).

A DEVELOPMENTAL OVERVIEW

The tiny newborn lies with fisted hands and tensed arms held close to the body; the 2-year-old confidently builds towers and solves puzzles. What has happened in the interval?

How a child handles toys, and what types of toys he enjoys at a particular age, follow fairly predictable patterns. Here's a quick overview of typical behavior. I do mean quick, and I do mean *typical.* Remember that your baby—every baby—has his own rate and schedule of development. The age guidelines here reflect averages, and no individual baby is exactly average.

The Early Months

A newborn has little control over his hands, or over arm movements, so he explores primarily by *looking* (see chapter 2, Early Eye-catchers).

He does automatically grasp something placed in his hand, though. This is a reflex that gives way to voluntary grasping over the next several months. For fun, you might give your newborn light things to hold. Right now he usually won't look at what he's holding, unless you draw his attention to it. Over the next few months he'll begin to coordinate eyes and hands to explore objects.

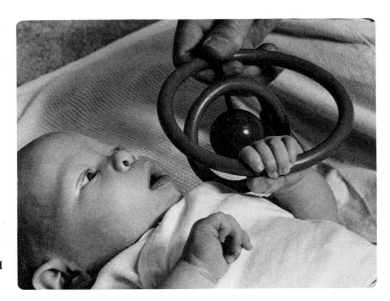

Babies a few weeks old automatically grasp any toy placed in their hands.

2 to 3 Months

Now your baby begins moving his arms with a bit of purpose. He enjoys batting a toy you dangle over him. Choose things that move and make sounds when he swats them. This batting and swatting are a preamble to the upcoming reaching with accuracy.

During this period a baby also begins to grasp toys voluntarily rather than merely as a reflex. He's a bit clumsy when making this transition—in fact, it may look like a step backward as he drops things he used to hold so tightly. At first he usually grasps with his entire hand, his four fingers moving as one (like he's wearing invisible mittens). Later he'll use the fingers differentially. Also, even though your baby holds things at will, he can't do much with them at this age.

4 Months

This is when a baby begins reaching for and grabbing toys with accuracy, especially when he lies on his back and you dangle something over his chest. Initially he's clumsy—he misjudges the distance between hand and object, or maybe he just can't get his hand to go exactly where he wants it

The 4-month-old reaches for toys you hold nearby.

to go. But practice makes perfect. He also uses both hands together. (Later he'll reach and grasp with one hand only.) The best toys are easy to grab and hold—remember that his hands are pretty tiny.

Mouthing is also popular, but most 4-month-olds lack the eye-hand coordination needed to bring a toy to mouth without help. Early handling, too, still consists largely of holding and dropping.

5 Months

Now mouthing is tops. At this age the baby easily brings things to the mouth, and keeps them there to extract every bit of information with his lips and tongue and cheeks. His mouth is an organ of touch, and at this age he can use it better than his hands to explore objects. Through mouthing he learns about size, shape, and texture as well as taste.

Handling skills are better at this age, too. A baby drops things less often. He also begins holding things with his fingers rather than his entire hand. But on the whole he relies more on his mouth than his fingers to explore a toy. The best playthings are light, easy to grasp, and easy to clean.

6 to 9 Months

This is real Age of Exploration, as mouthing (although still popular) takes backseat to handling. A baby reaches for and grasps a toy with no problem. And once he has it in hand, he tries everything with it: shaking, waving, pulling, stretching, poking, folding, twisting. . . . He uses his entire hand, or just a few fingers if he wishes. It's amazing all the things he'll try with almost any object he gets his hands on.

A baby this age explores one object at a time, so one-piece toys are best. (However, if the toy has moving parts attached to one another, even better!) Successful toys move, change shape, and make intriguing sounds when he explores them. In fact, the more ways a toy responds to his handling, the more he enjoys it.

Near the end of this period he also likes exploring small parts inside larger ones, so hand-held transparent toys are favorites, too.

From 6 to about 9 months, your baby loves toys that move, make sounds, and change shape as he plays.

10 to 12 Months

Crawling is such a thrill (new freedom!) that most beginning crawlers practically ignore handling objects for a spell. Don't be surprised if you see a temporary lull in toy interests.

The 10- to 12-monther still enjoys shaking, pulling, and probing the one-piece manipulatives so popular the past few months, but he also starts fancying toys that have several separate parts. Right now he tries some preliminary ways of relating two parts, such as knocking them together, or holding them side by side to inspect their similarities and differences.

Grasping skills are so well developed that by this age most babies can pick up a small object between the thumb and forefinger (this is called the *pincer* grasp). Take heed, though—small objects are dangerous because they'll go right into the mouth!

12 to 18 Months

The age of multipart toys. The young toddler tries all kinds of experiments—filling a container with smaller objects and dumping them out again, fitting rings over a spindle, nesting a set of cups inside one another, stacking up blocks, fitting two objects together and pulling them apart, solving simple puzzles.

Toddlers like toys with parts that can be stacked, nested, fitted together several different ways.

What follows this? A slackening interest in exploring objects and the ways they relate for their own sake; a burgeoning interest in using objects to build things, or in fantasy play. Young children enjoy other toys and activities, too, like riding and sliding and looking at books and hugging a lovey. All those are covered in different chapters.

BATTING AND SWATTING

Dangle a toy tantalizingly near your 2-month-old's hands. He spots it. Eyes widen. He gets excited, starts moving around, waves his fists haphazardly and—*bam!* He hits the toy. It moves. It makes sounds! He gets excited all over, waves his fists—*bam!* Over and over. What baby power.

Does a 2-month-old deliberately hit the dangling toy? Does he realize that *he's* making the toy move and make sounds? That's debatable. Some psychologists believe it's a matter of circumstance. That is, the hanging toy excites the baby, in his excitement he moves about and accidentally hits it, the toy's sound and motion excite the baby all over again so that he moves and hits it . . . and the cycle goes on. All the baby knows is that he moves around and the toy moves around, like magic, with no direct connection between the two events.

Other researchers give a baby more credit. They believe that he has some elementary understanding of the relationship between his actions and the toy's, and his hitting is more deliberate.

But it doesn't really matter. Most 2- to 3-month-olds *like* swatting at a dangling toy. It's also early eye-hand coordination practice, and an important step toward reaching and grasping with accuracy, which will develop over the next several months.

Some Guidelines for Batting

1. Lay your baby on his back—on your lap, the sofa, the changing table, a pad on the floor. Dangle a toy *just a few inches* above his fist and encourage him to bat it. You may think this is too close, but it's not. Is he having a little trouble getting started? Tap the toy against his fist a few times.

2. When he's a bit more skillful, he'll bat at toys a little further away. He might also like batting toys when he's sitting in your lap or an infant seat and you dangle an object out in front of him.

3. Good batting toys include anything that:

   ○ is colorful—to attract your baby's attention in the first place;

   ○ is fairly light;

   ○ is large enough for your baby to hit easily; and

   ○ makes sounds when hit.

   Dangle the toy from your fingers or a short piece of yarn. Remember—it should swing fairly freely.

4. For batting on the go, tie a toy across the carriage with a piece of inch-thick elastic strap.

This homemade Bat-a-Bag is great for batting games on the floor, lap, or infant seat. Hold one end of the strap in each hand and dangle the bag portion near your baby's fists. The straps let you tie it across the carriage, too.

○ **BAT-A-BAG**

Ideal Intro Age: 2 Months
Age Range: 2 to 4 Months
FOR SUPERVISED PLAY ONLY

Tools & Materials

   ○ Piece of colorful, patterned cloth, about 10″ × 10″

   ○ Piece of 1″ wide elastic strap, about 24″ long

   ○ Small plastic container with lid (like an empty aspirin bottle) with a few dried beans, screws, or other rattling soundmakers inside

○ Crumpled paper, for stuffing

○ Sewing machine or needle and thread

Directions

1. Fold the fabric in half, with the patterned sides (if any) facing each other. Stitch closed the two short sides, making a long pouch.
2. Turn this pouch patterned-side out again and stuff with the aspirin bottle and crumpled paper.
3. Position the elastic strap along the open edge of the pouch as shown on page 37. Stitch them together, simultaneously closing the bag and attaching the strap.

HINT: If you plan to hang this toy across your baby's carriage, measure the carriage before starting to determine the length strap you need. The strap must span the carriage with enough left over to tie onto either side.

SAFETY NOTE: This toy is for batting only. The straps make it dangerous for a baby to play with if it's not attached to something or held by a parent.

Play Gyms

A crib or cradle gym is the traditional batting-reaching toy for the 2- to 5-month old. Essentially, this is some kind of support (a rod, an arch) that spans the crib, and some toys (things to bat, grasp, pull on) that hang from it. There are a few good gyms on the market as of this writing. The best share these features:

○ Easy adjustability! You'll want to hang the toys very low, close to your 2- or 3-month-old's hands for batting, a little further away when he starts reaching with a purpose.

○ The hanging toys should swing and make sounds when hit.

○ At least some of the hanging toys should have a ring or handle that your baby can grasp easily.

SAFETY NOTE: *Never* tie any object across your baby's carriage, crib, or playpen once he can sit up or push up on hands and knees (usually at around 5 or 6 months). He might get tangled in it—with disastrous and heartbreaking results.

What about toys to bat and reach for out of the crib? After all, your baby usually prefers being near you when he's awake. If you're just too busy at the moment to play batting and reaching games, perch him (in his infant seat) in this homemade Play Box. It's a great place to practice reaching, grasping, and other aspects of eye-hand coordination.

PLAY BOX

Ideal Intro Age: 3 Months
Age Range: 3 to 6 Months
FOR SUPERVISED PLAY ONLY

Tools & Materials

- ○ Large cardboard box

- ○ Short pieces of elastic strap or thick, soft yarn

- ○ Small hand toys: rattles, things on rings, squeak toys, etc.

- ○ Packing or wrapping tape, at least 1″ wide (optional)

- ○ Sharp knife or scissors

The homemade Play Box is a portable gym that puts toys near your baby.

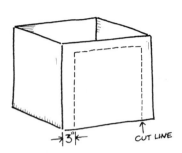 

3"   CUT LINE

Directions

1. Cut all the flaps off the top of the box.
2. Cut a large opening in one side, as shown. Make sure you leave at least a three-inch cardboard frame around the three sides, to give the box strength.
3. If these cut surfaces are rough, line them with tape.
4. From the top "arch" over the opening, hang a few hand toys on short pieces of elastic or yarn (six-inch maximum; your baby might get tangled in longer pieces).
5. Sit your baby in his infant seat, then place him seat and all into the box. Slide him forward far enough through the opening so that he can easily reach the dangling toys. What's nice about this setup is that the weight of your baby and the infant seat hold the box steady as he plays.

HINTS

○ Hang things on the inside sides of the box for your baby to look at: a picture cut from a magazine (run tape around all 4 sides of the picture so your baby can't rip it off) or a homemade Eye Target, page 19. Or cut a window in one side.

○ Invite older brother or sister to beautify this box with crayons or markers or wrapping paper they can glue on.

○ You should probably discontinue using the Play Box when your baby can pull the hanging toys hard enough to threaten the walls with collapse.

SAFETY NOTE: Keep an eye on your baby any time he's in his infant seat, whether or not he's using his Play Box. He might get so active that he topples himself, and needs you to free him again. Also, as a general rule, *never* leave your baby in his infant seat on a table or kitchen counter or other raised surface. He just might squirm over.

REACHING & GRABBING GAMES

Starting around 4 months or so, your baby no longer just bats randomly at dangling toys. He reaches deliberately with open hands. And once he grabs something, he pulls on it or waves it about to make sounds. Try some reach-and-grab games. These are played just like the earlier batting games, except that the toys should have handles, rings, or other protrusions your baby can grasp easily.

Let your baby reach for a dangling toy when lying on his back. When he grabs it, pull back slightly for some tug-of-war.

Sit your baby in your lap and dangle a toy out in front of him. Or dangle it to one side. Or up a little above his head, so he really has to stretch. But don't make it too hard to grab the toy—you want to challenge, not frustrate. And hold him securely so he doesn't tumble off your lap in his eagerness.

The homemade Grabbable Glove has plenty of convenient "handles," and the strap lets you dangle it over your baby, or even tie it onto the crib side, crib gym, or stroller.

GRABBABLE GLOVE

A super simple toy for reaching, grasping, exploring.
Ideal Intro Age: 4 Months
Age Range: 3 to 9 Months

Use the homemade Grabbable Glove for reaching and grasping games.

Tools & Materials

- Colorful, small fabric glove (machine washable)
- Stuffing: Polyester fiberfill, old nylons, etc. (machine washable)
- Piece of elastic strap, no more than 6″ long
- Needle and thread or sewing machine

Directions

1. Stuff the glove tightly; make sure you force stuffing into the fingers and thumb.
2. Sew it closed.
3. Stitch on the strap, as shown.

Your baby will grab almost any object within reach, so make sure he doesn't have access to cups of hot liquids, small or sharp objects, or anything else that could be dangerous. He'll grab *you*: hair, face, eyeglasses, and jewelry. Many mothers I know find it convenient to switch from pierced earrings to clip-ons for the next several months. And when he gives a really nasty tug on your hair or beard, gently pry open his little hand with a mild admonishment: "No—that hurts. Be gentle." He'll get the message over time.

ACTIVE HANDS (AND MOUTH)!

Six months old already. For the next few months, as your baby enjoys this so-named Age of Exploration, he delights in playing with all kinds of toys.

A number of dramatic behavioral advances make this such a rich play era. One, your baby has developed good eye-hand coordination; he now reaches for objects quickly and surely. Two, his grasping skills are vastly improved, so he uses fingers (as well as mouth) to explore the intricacies of playthings. Three, his arm skills, too, are advanced. Now he can deliberately wave and shake objects to see what happens, or stretch an elastic toy between both hands, or pound a favorite rattle against the floor to make as much noise as he can. All these arm and hand skills enable him to learn more about the properties of objects. And four, now he can sit all by himself. Among other things, this frees his hands and arms for play. And since he can't yet crawl, he's content to stay in one place, playing with anything within reach. When you combine all the above skills, they spell new play opportunities.

Most of the one-piece baby toys you find in stores are really designed for this age; you have a vast selection from which to choose. The best toys inspire and respond to several skills: shaking, waving, poking, and so forth. And remember that sounds and movement are the most powerful rewards for this age.

As you shop, keep these added guidelines in mind.

○ Toys for this age should be one-piece, since a baby explores just one thing at a time. In fact, even if you give him a set of rattles that fit together, chances are he explores one, then the other, but doesn't try to relate them. Look for toys that have a few parts attached to one another, or that are hinged, so that as your baby plays, the toy flops around and changes shape.

○ A toy should be easy for your baby to get hold of, especially when he accidentally drops it—which he will, constantly. Toys that lie perfectly flat on the floor will be hard for him to pick up. Look for those in which some portion serves as a handle that is raised off the floor.

○ Plastic is an excellent material for this age. Most plastics are strong, light, and easy to wash (remember that your baby will mouth everything he gets his hands on). Wood is less successful, since it can splinter and tends to be heavy. Fabric toys are also good, provided that they are easy to grasp, flop about, and make sounds when your baby plays—and provided that they are machine washable. The homemade Triple Mittens and Talking Sock fit these criteria.

SAFETY NOTE: Toys should be free of sharp edges, holes small enough to trap a finger, or pinch points. If the toy has a squeaker, make sure it is so firmly attached that *you* can't pick it out. (If your baby does, he might choke on it.) Stuffed toys should have well-sewn seams, so that your baby can't get to the stuffing (and sometimes soundmakers) inside. And small features like eyes and decorations should, again, be so firmly attached that you can't pick them off. For this age group, embroidered or printed faces on soft toys are the safest.

TRIPLE MITTENS

This soft toy has plenty of parts for grasping and chewing on; and the protruding thumbs make it simple to pick up again when dropped.
Ideal Intro Age: 6 Months
Age Range: 4 to 12 Months

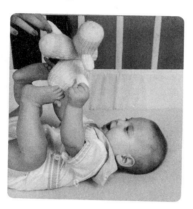

Homemade Triple Mittens is easy to grasp, pick up, chew on.

Tools & Materials

- 3 small child's mittens (machine washable)

- Stuffing material: polyester fiberfill, old stockings, etc. (machine washable), or 1 or 2 Mylar balloons* (deflated)

- Sewing machine or needle and thread

Directions

1. Stuff each mitten well with either Mylar or the stuffing material, leaving about one-half inch unstuffed at the wrist.

*Mylar (metallized polyester film) is a thick, shiny, cellophanelike material that's sometimes used to make helium-filled balloons. It is very strong and withstands machine washing. And it crackles tantalizingly when squeezed.

2. Sew the mittens closed where the stuffing ends.
3. Sandwich the mittens together as shown, alternating the direction in which the thumbs point, and sew all three together at the wrists.

HINTS

○ Machine wash in cold water and line dry. The Mylar might melt at high temperatures.

○ Save the remaining mitten to make a Beanbag, page 63.

Play Tips

Use these Triple Mittens in reach-and-grab games, too. Or when baby is older, this is a great soft "ball" for tossing.

TALKING SOCK

Divide a sock into three or four sections—each one stuffed with a different type of soundmaker. The resulting squeezable, shakable soft toy flops about as baby plays.
Ideal Intro Age: 6 Months
Age Range: 6 to 12 Months

The homemade Talking Sock rewards play with movement and plenty of sounds.

Tools & Materials

○ Woman's long cotton sock (with a perky design)

○ Material that crackles when you squeeze and handle it; for example, some types of plastic shopping bags, cellophane candy wrappers, a Mylar balloon, (deflated). See note on p. 45.

○ Small squeak toy

○ Small rattle: such as a ball or ring with beads or other soundmakers inside

○ Strong thread (like embroidery thread)

Directions

1. Stuff the toe of the sock with the crackly material. To keep it in place, loop a piece of embroidery thread around the sock a few times, then pull *tight* and tie with a double knot. Snip off the ends of the thread at the knot.

2. Next, stuff the rattle in the open sock, above the crackly material, and trap it in place with the thread, as above.
3. Next, stuff the squeak toy in the sock and tie in place.
4. If there is any empty sock left, stuff the remaining portion with more crunchy material (or even old nylons), and close the top with a few loops of embroidery thread.

HINT: When it's time to wash this toy, snip through the thread loops, remove the contents, wash the sock, and stuff again.

SAFETY NOTE: Be sure you put the rattle (which is hard) in the middle of the sock, as described. If it's in one end, your child might bonk himself with it as he waves the toy around by the other end.

Activity Centers

By definition, an activity center (usually called a Busy Box, although that's a brand name) mounts on the side of the crib, and offers your child doors to open, knobs to twist, geegaws to slide, and so on. The best ones are pretty good toys—for the right age. Although most are marked for introduction at 6 months (or even younger), I've found that few children really play with an activity center before 9 or 10 months. However, they continue to enjoy this type of toy well into toddlerhood.

In fact, in a survey of 50 homes of toddlers, in which parents were asked to name their child's ten favorite toys, an activity center was the #1 choice for young toddlers.

Paper Play

Plain old paper is a favorite toy for the Explorer—it's easy to grasp, easy to crumple, fun to toss and tear. One baby I know delighted himself for an hour with an out-dated telephone directory. Remember, though, always to supervise paper play; your baby might try to swallow—and consequently choke on—a ripped bit.

A discarded phone book can keep your baby happily occupied (but be sure to supervise).

Explorer's Pool

The wading pool is good for dry play indoors, too. Instead of water, fill it with several tantalizing toys, then your baby. The pool keeps everything clean and close at hand (remember—your baby will drop things a lot).

PLAY TIPS

○ Baby tosses a toy out of the pool . . . you retrieve it . . . he tosses it again . . . you retrieve it . . . he tosses again . . . you encourage him to toss *all* the toys out. Then you fill the pool for another round.

○ If you're game, empty out the toys and fill the pool with crumpled newspaper for your baby to thrash around in. Keep in mind that he'll get dirty from the print, so be prepared with a bath. And stay close by to make sure he doesn't eat the paper.

○ Or fill the pool with boulders of crumpled wrapping paper. Be sure the type of paper is "limp" enough so that it doesn't form sharp corners when compressed.

SAFETY NOTE: It's best to supervise when your baby is in his Explorer's Pool, to make sure he doesn't climb or tumble out head first.

Play on the Go

For play on the go, attach a favorite toy to your baby's stroller or carseat. Use a short piece of elastic strap or thick soft yarn (six-inch maximum—he might get tangled in a longer piece).

SAFETY NOTE: Never tie a toy—even a pacifier—on a loop of string and put it around your baby's neck, like a necklace. He could get the cord caught on something, and strangle.

PEEKABOO

Starting around 6 months, most babies adore games of peekaboo. The versions are endless, but the structure is the same: a person "disappears," then reappears accompanied by the jolly "Peekaboo, I see you!" cry.

○ Baby's in his crib, you're outside it. Duck out of sight, then pop back into view: "Peekaboo, I see you."

○ Baby's lying on your lap, facing you. Cover your eyes with your hands: "Where did Paul go? I can't see Paul." Away come your hands and, "There he is! Peekaboo, I see you." For a twist, help baby cover your eyes with *his* hands.

○ When he's fairly familiar with this game, your baby might like you to cover his eyes with your hand. Or help him cover his eyes with his own hands. Near the end of this first year, he might even cover and uncover his eyes all by himself. Or he'll hold his hands over his eyes and wait for you to pull them away with the "peekaboo" exclamation.

○ Hide your face behind a toy, such as an Eye Target, page 19, or the Picture Parade, page 22.

○ Cover your head with a diaper or towel, pause a second, pull it off.

Peekaboo! After a few rounds, your baby might like to snatch away the cover himself.

○ When your baby's 9 or so months old, try hiding *his* head under a diaper. (Being covered up usually frightens younger babies.) Make sure he's in a playful mood; initially he might not fancy the surprise of being covered even at this age. Smile and giggle at the unveiling to let him know this is indeed a game. Once he catches on, he'll probably take the upper hand, covering his face all by himself and waiting for you to grab the diaper away (or doing it himself).

○ For giant-sized family games, one parent and baby hide under a blanket, the other parent is the unveiler.

Toddler Games

Peekaboo games are still popular during the toddler years; and now that your child can walk, they can take on larger dimensions. For example, try some games of hide-and-seek—you hide somewhere in a room (behind a sofa or curtain) and call out for your toddler to find you.

Let your novice seeker watch you hide the first few times. He may need this clue to your whereabouts to be a successful sleuth. Also, he might not understand the purpose of the game right away—that is, to find you again. So make it easy. In fact, you'll probably need to hide in the same room that he's in.

When both parents can play (or maybe a parent and an older sibling), try some real hide-and-seek games. One parent hides somewhere in the house or yard, the other parent and toddler join forces to seek the missing player. Through this partnership your toddler picks up the game's fundamentals, and will later search for the hidden player without a parent's side-by-side guidance. Reverse roles. This time, toddler and one parent hide somewhere, the other parent seeks. Giggles and conspiratorial whispers ("This is the best spot—Mom'll never look here") add to the fun.

For a special place to hide, and for all kinds of peeking play, make a special Peeking House.

PEEKING HOUSE

A scaled-up twist on a favorite game.
Ideal Intro Age: 15 Months
Age Range: 15 to 36 Months

Tools & Materials

- Large cardboard carton

- Packing or wrapping tape (optional)

- Scissors or sharp knife

Directions

1. Cut off one of the long sides of the box.
2. On the remaining sides, cut several peep holes—different sizes and shapes if you like. Just make sure that every hole is too small for your child to fit his head through.
3. Cover any rough edges with tape, to prevent scratches.

Decorate your homemade Peeking House any way you wish.

HINT: Your older child—or even your toddler, if he's into crayons and markers—can decorate the box.

Play Tip

Stand the box up, with the open side to the back. Your toddler sneaks behind and peekaboos out. You peekaboo right back. Or he might want to hide *under* the box and peek out.

Peekaboo and Separation Anxiety

One reason peekaboo is so popular is that it links nicely to a facet of emotional development.

Starting sometime after 6 months, many babies become quite distressed when separated from their parents. It doesn't matter whether you're going out for the evening or just down to the laundry room—as soon as you make a move for the door your baby is clingy and grief stricken.

This behavior is commonly called *separation anxiety*. It might baffle you, especially if your baby used to let you come and go without much

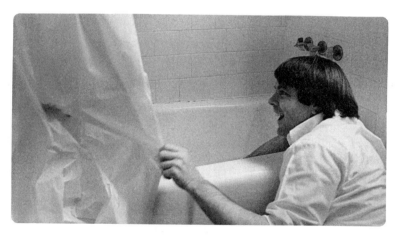

Peekaboo games may help your child work through separation anxiety.

notice. There are times it probably vexes you, too, when you're in a hurry and your baby won't let you go.

It's natural that you might mutter to yourself, "This is ridiculous—he knows I'm coming back soon."

But, in a way he doesn't.

By 6 or 7 months he *does* realize how much he loves and needs you—a positive step in your lifelong love affair. But here's the rub. Just as he's realizing his dependence on you, he also begins realizing that you can leave, that you're not always available. And when you're not there, he feels abandoned. It's a big realization for such a small, relatively helpless person!

Nor does he truly realize you will always return. At this age a baby doesn't fully understand *object permanence:* that things, including people, that disappear can reappear. (Understanding of this concept develops during the latter half of this year. You can help your baby learn with peekaboo and the Hiding & Finding Toys games in the next section.) In his mind, an object ceases to exist once it leaves his sight. So each time you leave, he can't really count on your reappearance. No wonder he feels anxious.

Through time and experience with your comings and goings (and with things disappearing and reappearing), your baby learns that you can, indeed, be depended on to come back. His separation anxiety will diminish, then disappear. He might go through similar spells during toddlerhood, too. As his love for you grows greater still, there are times your absence will make him insecure.

Peekaboo is really a way of acting out separations and reunions, but in a pleasant, nonthreatening context. It's also a situation your baby helps control (unlike your real leavings). It's fun to control things yourself when so much of your life is controlled by others. Some psychologists believe that peekaboo games can even help a baby work through some of his anxiety.

HIDING & FINDING TOYS

You hide a toy, your baby finds it. "Good for you, clever Jason!" you say. He's so proud of himself.

Like peekaboo, this basic game has endless varieties, and like peekaboo, it can help your child understand an important concept—object permanence. And, again like peekaboo, it's fun.

Most babies start to enjoy hiding-and-finding games at around 8 or 9 months, the typical age when they're beginning to grasp object permanence. A younger baby typically loses interest in a toy that leaves his sight. Make sure your baby watches you hide the toy. Otherwise he won't understand that he's supposed to find it again. And if your baby is new to this game, you might leave part of the hidden toy exposed, as a not-so-subtle clue.

Good Hiding Places

○ Under something—diaper, towel, inverted plastic bowl or small box, your hands, etc.

○ Inside something—a box with a flip-up top (like a cigar box) or a loosely fitting top (like a shoebox), a large boot, a cooking pot with matching lid, etc.

○ Behind something—your back (baby crawls around you to retrieve the hidden toy).

Toddler Games

1. Loosely wrap a toy in a piece of paper (especially regular wrapping paper). Let your child open his "present." Add to the festivities with a chorus of "Happy Birthday."
2. Take two different colored hand towels. Hide a toy under one of them. Can your toddler find it easily? Try three towels.

3. Take two containers (such as the largest cups from a set of stacking/nesting cups). Hide a small toy under one of them. Can your toddler find it easily? Shuffle the cups around, like the old shell game.

EXPLORING TEXTURES

Texture, just like sound and color, is a physical property of an object, and one that most babies enjoy exploring. Your baby will probably stroke and finger his toys (especially cloth ones), the carpet, your clothing, almost anything he gets his hands on. Add variety with these texture toys and games.

1. Take your baby on a "texture tour" of your home. Let him feel things like curtains, water rushing from a tap, bumpy bedspreads, fluffy towels. Try to describe the textures as best you can (some will really tax your vocabulary and imagination).
2. Try a "texture walk" outdoors, too, pausing frequently so your child can feel the rough bark of trees, smooth leaves, prickly grass shoots, brick walls, signposts. . . .

   The following homemade texture toys give him a variety of textures to explore at a sitting.

TOUCHABLE GLOVE

You wear this glove, your baby explores each textured finger.
Ideal Intro Age: 6 Months
Age Range: 6 to 12 Months

Tools & Materials

○ Large glove

○ Fabric scraps—choose a variety of textures

○ Needle and thread

The homemade Touchable Glove gives your baby five textures to explore at once.

Directions

Sew a scrap of fabric firmly onto each of the glove's fingers.

Play Tips

Use this glove to give your baby a textury massage.

TEXTURE CARDS

Ideal Intro Age: 9 Months (a younger baby would probably rather chew these cards than feel them)
Age Range: 9 to 36 Months

Talk about the different textures on these homemade Texture Cards.

Tools & Materials

- Several 5″ × 8″ file cards (or other pieces of cardboard)
- The same number of different-textured fabric scraps: corduroy, terrycloth, flannel, dotted swiss, felt, velvet, etc.
- Short piece of thick, soft yarn
- White household glue
- Scissors and, if available, hole punch

Directions

1. Glue a different fabric on each card, covering it completely. Trim off any excess.
2. Punch or poke a hole in the upper right hand corner of each card; tie the cards together loosely with a small loop of yarn.

SAFETY NOTE: Supervise play if your baby is under a year old. He might try to tear off the fabric and put it (or the card) into his mouth.

TEXTURE BOOK

Ideal Intro Age: 12 Months
Age Range: 12 to 36 Months

Tools & Materials

- Blank scrapbook; buy one or make one from sheets of cardboard

A homemade Texture Book is great for your toddler.

- Textured materials; some suggestions:

  - Fabric scraps

  - Fine-grained sandpaper

  - Short pieces of thick, soft yarn

  - Squares of corrugated cardboard

  - Old greeting cards with glitter or embossed surfaces

  - Textured wallpaper samples (especially flocked)

- White household glue

Directions

Glue a few textured objects on each page of the book.

SAFETY NOTE: Avoid small things (like cotton balls) that might be a hazard if your toddler should rip them off a page.

SURPRISE TOUCH BOX

Here's a surprise way your older toddler can explore objects just by touch. Just put a textured object inside the Surprise Touch Box and replace the lid. Your child reaches in through the hole and feels it. You might even ask him to guess what he's touching.

Ideal Intro Age: 24 Months
Age Range: 24 to 36 Months

Tools & Materials

- Adult-sized shoe box with lid

- Cloth tape

- Scissors

With this homemade Surprise Touch Box, your toddler explores objects just by feel.

Directions

1. Cut a tunnel-shaped opening in one end of the box. Make sure it is large enough to easily accommodate your child's hand.
2. Line the cut edges with tape to prevent scratches.

PUTTING IT TOGETHER

At some point between 9 and 12 months, your baby no longer plays with one thing at a time. Maybe he hits two rattling toys together to see what happens. Or he puts a small object into a larger one. This is a beginning. Over the next year or so he'll try all kinds of things, like building towers (and knocking them over), filling a container and emptying it again, fitting things together, solving simple puzzles . . . all kinds of things. Now he prefers toys that have several different pieces.

One reason he loves multipart playthings is because the one-year-old is fascinated with organization and connection—what goes with what.

At this age your child is making more sense out of the world. He realizes that there is a logical order to many things. For example, he's beginning to understand what familiar objects are used for—a cup is for drinking out of, shoes are for wearing on the feet. He also realizes that certain objects belong in particular places—his socks go in the dresser, books and toys on the nursery shelves. (Unfortunately for you, he probably won't put his things away at this age, but he is beginning to understand where they should go.)

Once your child begins talking, you'll notice this fascination even more clearly. He loves to connect words with objects, and will constantly be asking you "What's dat?" He also delights in connecting people with their possessions, and will croon on about Daddy's shoes and Mommy's shoes and "My shoes!"

His interest in organization naturally extends to his play. That's why he spends countless hours exploring the ways in which he can organize the parts of a toy: stack them, nest them, fit them inside or under one another. Through these experiments he also learns important concepts like size differences and spatial concepts (inside, under, on top of), especially when you supply the appropriate words as you and he play: "Good for you—you put the block inside the box." And in the bargain, he practices precise eye-hand coordination.

However, he hasn't left behind totally the play of the baby months. He still shakes and mouths and otherwise explores objects. Many favorite baby toys of the past few months continue to delight him.

Here are some of the most popular multipart toys and games (and some things you can make, too).

Fill & Dump

The favorite early activity is putting objects into some kind of container, taking or dumping them out, then repeating the process—sometimes for long stretches. This Fill & Dump play is fairly mistakeproof; the opening in the container is much larger than the objects that go inside. It's also a forerunner of fitting things together, like a shape sorter, that require more precision.

GOOD CONTAINERS Plastic mixing bowl, small cardboard box, large Tupperware-type plastic food storage containers, empty coffee can (make sure the cut edge isn't sharp!).

GOOD FILLERS Plastic pop beads, coasters (an absolute favorite), balls, blocks, rattles, and other favorite small baby toys.

GOOD GAMES

A coffee can and coasters are super Fill & Dump toys.

1. Try Fill & Dump on a grander scale, with a big box or plastic laundry basket and an assortment of good-sized toys, especially stuffed animals. Have a race—you toss toys into the box, your toddler throws them out as quickly as he can.

2. A great game for clean-up time: Encourage your toddler to put large toys into an even larger container. Since he has to stand up to play, and maybe even toddle around the room to gather ammunition, his whole body is involved in the game.

GOOD HOMEMADE TOYS These homemade Fill & Dump toys—Sock Beanbags, Container Bank, Posting Cards—are designed for different skill levels.

SOCK BEANBAGS

Homemade Sock Beanbags are great for Fill & Dump. They're easy to pick up because they "mold" to your toddler's hand.
Ideal Intro Age: 12 Months
Age Range: 12 to 36 Months

Tools & Materials

For each beanbag:

- Sturdy child's sock
- Dried beans
- Scissors
- Needle and thread or sewing machine

Directions

1. Fill the foot section of a sock with beans.
2. Snip off the remaining portion of the sock about one inch above the beans.
3. Turn the cut edges inside the sock (this will prevent ravelling) and sew the sock closed. Use a double or triple row of stitches to make sure the beans can't escape; if your toddler gets his hands on them he might swallow them or stuff them up his nose.

HINT: Instead of a sock, use a child's mitten.

Play Tips

- Give your baby a few Sock Beanbags and a plastic mixing bowl or a small cardboard box.

- These beanbags are also good stacking toys, because they sit on top of one another any way your toddler puts them.

- He can also use them as tossing toys in the homemade Target Toss, page 113.

○ 63 ○

CONTAINER BANK

This is a favorite because toddlers love the challenge of fitting things through a slot, and because the coasters make such a terrific clanking sound when they hit the metal coffee can. (See Safety Note!) Supervise play the first few times to make sure your toddler knows how to remove the lid once he has inserted the coasters.

Ideal Intro Age: 15 Months
Age Range: 15 to 30 Months

Tools & Materials

- Large, empty coffee can with plastic lid

- Set of coasters

- Cloth adhesive tape (optional)

- Sharp knife

Directions

In the plastic lid, cut a slot long and wide enough for the coasters to fit through easily. Line the slot with adhesive tape if the edges are sharp.

SAFETY NOTE: If the coffee can has a sharp edge where the metal lid was cut off, hammer it smooth. If you can't, discard the coffee can and use a plastic food storage container. It won't make as much noise, but it'll be fun just the same. Also, the coasters should be at least two inches in diameter; this size, at least according to toy safety standards, is too large to fit entirely into your toddler's mouth. If you use smaller coasters or other discs, it's best to supervise play.

POSTING CARDS

This Fill & Dump game uses playing cards—favorites of most older toddlers—that give you plenty of opportunities for reinforcing other skills.
Ideal Intro Age: 18 Months
Age Range: 18 to 36 Months

You and your toddler can play all sorts of Fill & Dump games with this homemade Posting Cards toy.

Tools & Materials

○ Deep adult-sized shoe box, with lid

○ Masking or packing tape, at least one inch wide

○ Deck of regular playing cards

○ Scissors or sharp knife

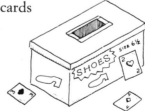

Directions

1. Cut a slot in the lid of the shoebox. It should be at least one inch longer than the cards, and at least one-half-inch wide.
2. Line the slot on all four sides with the tape to prevent rips.

Play Tips

From 18 Months:

○ Show your toddler how to insert cards through the slot one by one, then how to open the box, dump out its contents, and start again. Make it fun; pretend you're mailing postcards to friends ("Let's mail this one to Granny Palmer"), or putting dollar bills into a bank ("Here goes another dollar into our account—soon we'll have enough to buy those silver sandals"), or casting ballots ("That's one more vote for you as the World's Best").

NOTE: You might give your toddler just a partial deck; inserting all 52 cards may be overwhelming.

○ Alternate turns: He inserts a card, you insert a card, he inserts a card. . . . This helps him learn social rules like taking turns.

From 24 Months:

○ Use just the aces, twos, and threes.

○ Help your toddler count the spots on each card before he inserts it. Great for early counting skills.

○ Lay all 12 cards face up on the floor. Pick up one card (say, a deuce), and ask your toddler to find all the other cards that have the same number of spots, then to insert them into the box.

○ Use a pack of children's Old Maid cards. (An Old Maid deck consists of matched pairs of objects, people, or animals.) Separate about six pairs from the deck and put them face up on the floor (mixed around so the pairs aren't together). Now, pick up a card, ask your toddler to find its mate, and then let him insert both into the box. Talk about the pictured objects, too.

Nesting toys help your toddler learn size differences and spatial relationships.

Nesting Toys

Nesting two containers (i.e., putting the smaller into the larger) that are close in size requires more dexterity and discrimination than simple Fill & Dump. You can buy sets of inexpensive plastic nesting cups; they're well worth it because they'll be used in all kinds of play, including water and sand. Choose cups that also stack securely on one another when inverted.

HINT: The first few times your toddler plays with nesting cups, he might prefer using just a few—say, the largest, the middle size, and the smallest. Add more as his skill increases.

SAFETY NOTE: The smallest cup in the set should be too large to fit into your toddler's mouth. If it can fit, throw it away.

Stacking Toys

These include anything from stacking/nesting cups to blocks that fit on top one another to beanbags to special stacking opportunities built into toys that have other purposes as well. Most toddlers love to stack toys into towers. And knock them down. And stack them up.

INDIVIDUAL DIFFERENCES In building towers, just like in playing with any of the toys in this chapter (and, really, throughout this book), each toddler has his own style. I've seen some who are too impatient (at first) to create tall ones. They stack up just two or three items—or even urge a parent to—then knock the short tower over and start again. Or they rush through building, no matter how high they go, just to get to the destruction phase. Other toddlers work slowly and methodically. These persistent builders often test how high they can go. Some get a little annoyed when the tower falls—or when you knock it over, even in play. So if your toddler doesn't seem interested in tower building, or rushes through it, or plods along, or gets angry when things don't go according to plan, don't worry; these are all natural responses.

A RESEARCH STUDY At what age does stacking begin? How high a tower is typical at any given age? These, obviously, depend on the toys, because some are easier to stack than others.

It seems that stacking (again, like most play with toys) requires a meshing of physical and mental skills. On the physical side, your child has to be able to place the second toy on top of the first *and* let go without knocking the toy off. That final step's the hard part, and one reason why early stacking attempts can be rather clumsy. I've found that toddlers are more successful if the stacking objects fit together loosely—say, a tapered end into a hollow—rather than merely rest on each other.

On the mental side, the child has to be able to conceive of vertical space, and realize that his towers, indeed, can go as high as his physical skills will allow. For a toddler whose play with toys has largely been horizontal, that's no small step.

Because developmental psychologists feel that conceiving of space vertically is an important developmental milestone, they've examined tower building in young children. One definitive study, conducted by Arnold Gesell more than 40 years ago, found the following:

At 12 Months:
- 16 percent of the toddlers built a tower two blocks high; none built a higher one.

At 18 Months:

o 100 percent of the children built two-block high towers;

o 92 percent built three-block towers;

o 77 percent built four-block towers;

o 44 percent built five-block towers;

o 27 percent built six-block towers.

At 24 Months:

o 100 percent built two- and three-block towers;

o 97 percent built four-block towers;

o 85 percent built five-block towers;

o 76 percent built six-block towers.

At 36 Months:

o 100 percent of the children built towers, two, three, and four blocks high;

o 97 percent built towers five and six blocks high.

These are only guidelines, though. Dr. Gesell used identical one-inch cubes—which, incidentally, are so small they're dangerous for a toddler to play with unsupervised. You're bound to see differences in your own child's skill based partly on the toys he uses.

Stacking Rings on a Spindle

A set of plastic donutlike rings that fit on a spindle is another traditional toy that's well worth buying, although not necessarily for the reasons for which it was originally designed.

The rings will get plenty of play by themselves—as teethers, tossers, small toys for Fill & Dump and Hiding & Finding Toys games. Yes, your toddler will probably place a few over the spindle (especially if you demonstrate and encourage), but rarely in order. The size difference from one ring to the next is just too fine for most toddlers to discriminate between. Don't expect perfection.

If your toddler likes trying, give him just three rings—largest, middle-sized, and smallest. Add more as skills improve.

HINT: A stacking rings set is also one of the single best toys for teaching colors. Most plastic versions are quite inexpensive, too.

Early Fitting Toys

In the toy store, you'll find lots of toddler items in which one part, often a character, fits into another—a car, a boat, some kind of base. These usually work well. They're even better if the figures can somehow fit together end to end.

In fact, fitting objects, like hollow pegs, together end to end is one of the most popular behaviors I've witnessed in our labs. Not too many toys incorporate this feature, so look hard.

Blocks and Construction

Wooden blocks usually are more popular after 24 months than before. The younger toddler is just as happy with all the other types of fitting-stacking-nesting toys described before. Some toddlers don't use blocks much before 36 months, except maybe at nursery school or the day-care center where blocks are part of the social milieu.

Some toddlers like simple construction-type toys at 24 months, but it really depends on the particular toy. It's best to buy a small set of some modular system to start. Then when your toddler proves his interest, expand the number of pieces.

GIANT HOMEMADE BLOCKS Toddlers of all ages do like large, light blocks, though, partly for building, partly for crawling over, partly for

using as chairs. And partly because the not-so-large toddler feels powerful and important merely carrying them. What a great accomplishment it is, too, to build massive structures when you're not yet very massive yourself. Most big blocks you can buy, though, are expensive—if you can find them at all. The Postal Box Blocks and Grocery Bag Blocks fill the void. And they provide plenty of play. Some suggested games:

From 15 Months:

○ Stack a few blocks into a tower for your toddler to knock over. *Kaboom!* Go faster . . . faster. Who's faster—the construction company or the demolition expert?

○ Help your toddler build his own towers, too. A great way to enhance eye-hand coordination.

From 18 Months:

○ You build a tower or wall; he bulldozes it flat on his favorite riding toy.

○ With enough blocks you can even build forts and fantasy hide-outs.

○ Your older toddler (or his older brother or sister) might like to decorate these finished blocks with crayons or (nontoxic!) felt-tipped markers.

SAFETY NOTE: Since these blocks are made with paper and tape, it's best to introduce them after your toddler is past the stage where he rips up and eats paper, or picks at and eats tape.

POSTAL BOX BLOCKS

Great cardboard blocks made from the large size mailing cartons for sale at the post office.
Ideal Intro Age: 18 Months
Age Range: 15 to 36 Months

Tools & Materials

For each block you need:

- Large mailing carton

- Plenty of newspaper

- Wrapping or packing tape

- Hammer (optional)

Directions

1. Assemble the flaps to form the bottom of the carton, and tape them in place.
2. Fill the box a little to overflowing with balls of crumpled newspaper (for added sturdiness), press the paper down, and tape the top flaps closed.
3. If the corners feel sharp, pound them smooth with the hammer.

GROCERY BAG BLOCKS

These large, lightweight, surprisingly durable, and *free* blocks won't hurt walls, furniture, or other children should your toddler toss them. Make plenty.
Ideal Intro Age: 18 Months
Age Range: 15 to 36 Months

Tools & Materials

For each block you need:

- Brown paper grocery bag
- Newspaper—about 14 double-page sheets
- Packing or wrapping tape

Directions

1. Lay the closed bag on a flat, hard surface, fold over the top about eight inches and crease *well.*
2. Open the bag, stand it up, and fill nearly to the top with crumpled newspaper balls.
3. Press down the crumpled paper, fold over the top of the bag on the crease line, and tape it closed.

These homemade giant Grocery Bag Blocks are light, durable, and packed with play possibilities.

HINT: Experiment with the number of newspaper balls you need to stuff a bag fairly firmly. It might be more or fewer than the recommended fourteen.

Play Tip

Hold your toddler's hand and help him kick a block like a ball. It won't roll away—so kick it again . . . and again. When he's a good kicker, race each other kicking blocks around the room.

Puzzles

Teachers swear by puzzles because, as teachers have pointed out, puzzle play has so many benefits:

- It builds eye-hand coordination.
- It helps develop concepts like size, shape, spatial orientation (which side is up?), and positional relationships between separate parts of an object or entire objects in a scene.
- It helps a child learn the component parts of an object, and how these separate parts make up the whole.
- It helps a child's intellectual skills like matching, sequencing, and one-to-one correspondence. These are among the foundations for learning to read, write, and solve mathematical problems.
- It helps a child learn to concentrate.

The forced correctness of a puzzle offers nice contrast to the freer-range toys that have no one way to use them correctly. The self-pacing and self-correcting character of puzzle play lets the child test, correct, and retest himself.

Toddler tray puzzles come in two main types:

- *Island puzzles,* in which each removable piece is a complete object that fits into its own well in the puzzle tray.
- *Jigsaw puzzle,* in which each piece is a component of a whole, and all the pieces fit into the same large, shallow well.

A toddler is usually ready for three- or four-piece island puzzles by about 18 months. He probably needs help completing it, though.

Simple jigsaw puzzles are usually introduced between 24 and 36 months.

When buying puzzles, keep these things in mind:

○ Look for sturdiness. Favorite puzzles are worked and reworked endlessly.

○ Pieces must be easy to remove. Knobs and other handles help.

○ In a jigsaw puzzle, each piece should be recognizable when removed from the frame. That is, on a "person" puzzle, the leg should look like a leg, not a misshapen blob.

HOMEMADE PEOPLE PUZZLES These can't match commercial ones in durability, but they make up for it in personality.

Initially this type of jigsaw puzzle may be hard for your child to complete, since it doesn't have a tray that helps him orient the pieces. But the familiarity of the subject will give him clues.

When you and your toddler play together, talk about the people in the puzzles: who they are (if a family member), the parts of the face and body, what they're wearing, what they might be holding. If the puzzle people are wearing uniforms, talk about these and the respective professions, too. And if the puzzle is your toddler's picture—well, you have plenty to talk about.

Homemade People Puzzles
can help your toddler
learn component parts of an
object—even himself.

○

PEOPLE PUZZLES

Ideal Intro Age: 24 Months
Age Range: 24 to 36 Months

Tools & Materials

○ Picture of a person, about 8″ × 10″; cut from a magazine—or get a regular snapshot of your toddler enlarged at the photography store and use it

○ Sheet of thin cardboard, same size

○ White household glue

○ Scissors

Directions

1. Coat the back of the picture with glue. (Easy way: Pour some glue into a saucer, dilute slightly with water, and paint onto the picture with a damp paper towel.) Attach to the cardboard.
2. When the glue dries, cut the picture into a few pieces.

HINT: Look for a large, simple picture; ideally, showing the whole person. Cut it out along natural breaks; that is, maybe divide into head, torso, and legs. These divisions give your toddler clues for reconstruction. Also, the cuts should be wavy lines so that the pieces slide together, not fit like traditional adult jigsaw pieces. Is the puzzle too easy? Cut into some more pieces. Is it too hard? Tape some pieces back together.

Cookie-cutter Puzzle

Most toddlers love holidays—especially Christmas or Chanukah or other end-of-the-year celebrations. If you have any plastic holiday-related cookie cutters, you can use them in a homemade island puzzle that will have special meaning.

This toy is recommended for 24 months because the shapes will probably be a little harder for your child to fit than traditional island puzzle pieces.

The familiar shapes of this homemade Cookie-cutter Puzzle give it special meaning.

COOKIE-CUTTER PUZZLE

Ideal Intro Age: 24 Months
Age Range: 24 to 36 Months

Tools & Materials

- Set of plastic cookie cutters; make sure they don't have sharp edges

- 2 sheets of corrugated or other fairly thick cardboard, about 8" × 10"; you can cut these from a large cardboard box

- Sheet of colored paper

- Pencil

o Mat knife (also called a hobby knife)

o White household glue

o Cellophane (Scotch) tape

Directions

1. Trace the cookie cutter shapes on one piece of cardboard.
2. Carefully cut them out, using the mat knife.
3. Sandwich the sheet of colored paper between the two sheets of cardboard, and glue all three together.
4. Run tape around the entire perimeter.

HINT: You can use foam core board instead of the cardboard; it's easy to cut and looks terrific. Ask for it at art supply stores.

EARLY ART SUPPLIES

Many toddlers 18 to 24 months and up enjoy crayons, play dough, and other basic art materials. At this age they're more interested in the process than the product, and in dabbling for a few minutes, not working industriously to create a masterpiece. In other words, it's not the time to ask your child to draw a landscape for you. And since toddlers aren't the most careful of creatures, you should stay by to confine his creative urges to the page rather than the wall.

The following materials suit most toddlers.

Crayons

Choose jumbo crayons about one-half-inch in diameter. These are easier for a toddler to hold (he usually grasps them like a drumstick), and less likely to break. The nonrolling type stay close at hand. Make sure crayons are nontoxic—your toddler will probably put them into his mouth.

When he does, remove the crayon while reminding him that crayons are for drawing with, not eating. He'll learn this rule after a few attempts.

Give your toddler large sheets of paper to draw on. Best is a giant pad, available at an art supply store—it holds the page steady and gives him plenty of room. You can keep single sheets stationary by taping them to the drawing surface—highchair tray or table top.

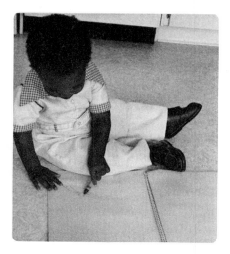

Give your toddler a big pad and jumbo crayons for his scribbling fun.

PLAY TIPS

○ Draw side by side. Many parents I know say that their toddlers love watching them draw, even if the parent isn't much of an artist. Ask him what he would like you to make.

○ Draw an object and ask your toddler to guess what it is.

○ Let your toddler color (really, scribble) in the shapes you've drawn.

Felt-tipped Markers

These beat crayons hands down—they make much more dramatic, colorful scribbles. But they are messier. Choose only nontoxic ones, and make sure your toddler no longer chews his art supplies. Supply *large* sheets of paper. It's also a good idea to protect the floor or table top with newspaper or a plastic cloth. He might miss his drawing pad on occasion.

Chalk

A chalk board and colored chalks make a nice, fairly clean set of art materials. Select the thickest chalks you can find. And expect breakage nonetheless.

Finger Paints

Finger paints are great for the toddler who loves to mess (as most toddlers do). Try giving yours this fake finger paint to see whether he likes the idea—and can be trusted to confine the sloppiness to a small setting.

○ Beat soap flakes (Ivory Snow, not powdered detergent) with water and some food coloring to make a smooth paste.

Your toddler can finger paint on a cookie sheet, the highchair tray, or directly on any table that sponges clean. Or let him paint in the bathtub—easy cleanups!

If he enjoys this, he's probably ready for the real thing. You can buy jars of finger paint (nontoxic) at toy and art supply stores. He can paint on any glossy paper, such as coated shelf paper or special finger paint paper sold in stores. Dampen the paper with a sponge, add a glop of paint (one color is fine), and stay close by to make sure he doesn't redecorate the room. When he's through, let the painting dry, then display it on the refrigerator (the favorite home art gallery).

Play Dough

At this age your toddler won't make specific objects. Rather, he'll love just squishing and squeezing and pounding the dough, or making shapes in it with objects like cookie cutters. Again, be sure to supervise so that dough doesn't end up in his hair—or worse.

○ **PLAY DOUGH**

Ideal Intro Age: 24 Months
Age Range: 24 to 36 Months

Tools & Materials

○ 2 cups flour   ○ ¾ cup salt

o ½ cup water o Food coloring

o 1 tablespoon salad oil o Mixing bowl

Directions

1. Mix together the flour and salt.
2. Add the water and oil, and knead well until it's smooth (about 10 minutes or so).
3. Add food coloring and knead until the color is fully blended.
4. Store in a plastic bag in the refrigerator.

HINT: You might need to add a bit more flour or water until the consistency is smooth but not sticky. Each time I make this dough, I have to vary the proportions slightly.

Poster Paints

These, too, can be fun but messy. Many parents I know confine painting to school. If you want to try at home, make sure your child wears a smock (one of your shirts, worn backwards, does the trick), and that the floor around the easel is protected with lots of newspaper or a plastic cloth. Or let your toddler paint outside. Drips and spills will be less destructive, and if the young artist is really sloppy, you can hose him off after paint time. A toddler does best with brushes that have bristles about an inch or more across. He might also like to use a piece of sponge instead of a brush. Make sure he doesn't chew it.

For a cleaner version of outdoor painting, give your toddler a real paint brush and a pail of water, and let him paint your house or sidewalk. It disappears—magic!

A brush and a bowl of water make a novel (and nondestructive!) outdoor "paint" set.

BALLPOINT PAINT PEN

This homemade art material is a fairly clean way to paint. In essence, it's a giant ballpoint pen. Your child can roll it across *large* sheets of paper to make dazzling scribbles.
Ideal Intro Age: 24 Months
Age Range: 24 to 36 Months

The homemade Ballpoint Paint Pen is made from an empty deodorant bottle.

Tools & Materials

- Empty roll-on deodorant bottle, with a removable top; wash it thoroughly

- Finger paint or poster paint

Directions

1. Pry the top off the bottle.
2. Fill with paint that you've diluted with water, and replace the top.

TO SUM UP

That's it for hands and heads. Of course, you and your child will undoubtedly devise your own toys and games—good for you! Now let's look at activities for the entire body. On to exercise.

ACTIVE PLAY & EXERCISE

Active play means kicking, sitting, crawling, walking and running, jumping, climbing and sliding, tossing a ball, riding a ride-on, slugging a punching bag. Psychologists generally call these the large muscle or *gross-motor skills,* in contrast to the *fine-motor skills* covered in Chapter 3, Activities for Hands (and Heads).

The younger the child, the more she welcomes your participation. The newborn has relatively little control over her large muscles, and looks to you for nearly all physical activity. As a baby develops skills—sitting, crawling, walking—she engages progressively in independent gross-motor play. In fact, unlike many of us adults, she rarely needs encouragement; the sheer joy of movement is inducement enough.

Even so, you play an important role in your child's large-muscle activities. She needs you to provide safe play spaces and appropriate equipment at the right age. She welcomes your help when she tackles a new task, from pulling to stand to taking those historic first steps. When she

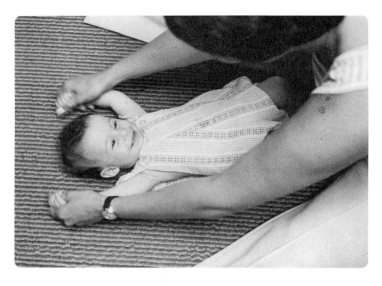

Baby exercises help build muscles, coordinate movements— and they're *fun*!

falters, your sympathy and encouragement can disspell momentary feelings of failure. And when she's successful, how she loves your praise. She welcomes the variety you can devise—new things to crawl through, to climb over, to slide down, to swat. Last but far from least, she likes playing all kinds of games with you. This chapter helps all of you enjoy *active play and exercise.*

LOVING TOUCHES

Touching and stroking are a form of communication. A baby picks up unspoken messages about her caregivers from the way she's handled, much the way we form impressions of people based on handshakes and embraces. Expressing your love through caring touch gives your baby a sense of security.

Most babies enjoy physical stimulation right from birth. A baby also *needs* a certain amount of touching, cuddling, and rocking for proper development. In the past, some institutionally-raised infants received proper food and other physical care but were rarely held. They often failed to thrive. You needn't worry about that, however. Your baby typically receives lots of physical stimulation during feeding (when she's held and rocked), bathing, and dressing, cuddling her and soothing her cries. If you're brand new parents, though, with all the things new parents think and worry about, you might overlook ways to add variety to these regular routines. Two very pleasant ways are massages and exercises.

Individual Differences

Babies differ in how much they like to be held and cuddled. Most welcome the close, secure contact, but some chafe at the seeming restraint unless very sleepy. Some babies, too, don't especially like to be stroked and massaged. If your baby isn't a cuddler, don't take it as a sign of personal rejection; it's just part of the personal style she was born with. She might prefer being rocked in a cradle or rocking infant seat.

Stroking & Massaging

End bathtime or a diaper change with a soothing massage. Gently and rhythmically rub or stroke your baby's back, stomach, and limbs. Use your bare hands, or add variety by wearing a soft glove or mitten. You might also try stroking your baby with a very soft artist's paintbrush, a large feather, or a cotton ball. Always watch her reaction to see whether she's enjoying these different sensations.

I recommend that you ask your baby's pediatrician before massaging with lotion or baby oil. Some babies have naturally oily skin and shouldn't have the additional moisture. Also, a young baby's pores often don't work properly (one reason she may get prickly heat in warm weather), and the lotion may clog them.

Baby Exercises

Even though your baby can't move her limbs with coordination, *you* can, with simple baby exercises. When she's on her stomach, hold her feet and help her do some frog kicks: Up (heels touch her bottom), out (legs straightened in a "V"), and back together. On her back you can bicycle her legs and stretch her arms.

Many parents and babies I know have developed their own set of baby exercise routines—and each is as individual as a parent-baby pair. The following simple exercises, best introduced after 1 month, will get you started. Make up more!

1. Bring your baby's hands together, cross them over her chest, then stretch them out to the sides.
2. Stretch both arms up past her head, then down to her sides.
3. Stretch one arm up, the other down, then alternate.
4. Do some knee bends: Both legs together, or alternating—one leg, then the other.
5. Touch baby's left hand to her right knee, then alternate.

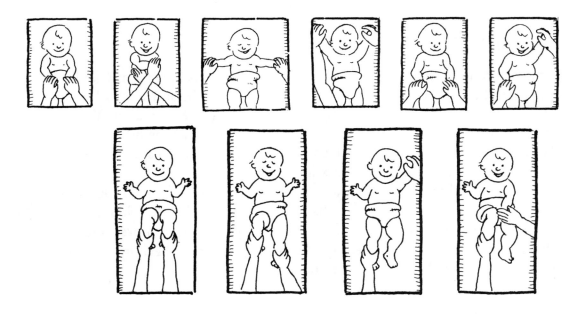

PLAY TIPS

○ Repeat a single exercise (say, deep knee bends) any number of times, then switch to another. Combine a series of separate exercises into a continuous routine.

○ Exercise on a soft surface—like the Exercise Porta-pad below.

○ Keep your movements gentle and smooth. Never jerk your baby into position. Let her set the pace, too, by watching her cues and reactions. Some babies like quiet exercising, others prefer more rigorous routines.

○ Sing or chant favorite nursery rhymes (or popular songs), and move your baby to the rhythm.

○ For more exercise ideas, talk to an instructor or join a baby exercise class. For information on classes in your area, contact your local Y, public library, community college, Red Cross, or groups (such as Lamaze) that sponsor childbirth education.

EXERCISE PORTA-PAD

A perfect place to do your baby exercises and a soft, clean spot for changing diapers wherever you and your baby may be.
Ideal Intro Age: 2 Months
Age Range: 2 to 18 Months

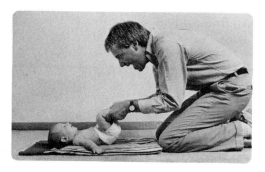

The perfect place for exercises? This homemade Exercise Porta-pad.

Tools & Materials

○ 1 patterned pillowcase (a dark one shows less dirt)

○ 2 or 3 thicknesses of quilt batting, in sheets the same size as the pillowcase (batting is available at fabric, sewing, and craft stores)

○ Piece of sturdy fabric ribbon, 16″ long

○ Sewing machine or needle and thread

Directions

1. Lay the batting sheets inside the pillowcase and sew it closed.
2. If you're using a sewing machine, run a row of stitches lengthwise and a row or two widthwise to hold the batting in place. Or, with needle and thread, add strong stitches in various spots across the pillowcase surface.

3. Attach the ribbon through its middle, as shown, making a pair of eight-inch straps.
4. To transport, roll the pad into a tube (starting from the short end without the straps), and tie it into a cylinder.

KICKING GAMES

By about 4 months, your baby can control her leg movements and loves to flail around and kick up her heels. Turn this into a fun exercise with the following game.

○ Your baby lies on her back—in her crib, on the changing table, in the middle of your bed, or on a mat on the floor. You dangle a large toy over her feet, encouraging her to give it some spirited kicks. Use an easy-to-hit target that swings and makes sounds— these rewards encourage her to keep on kicking. You might want to tap the toy against her feet a few times to start the play.

The perfect toy? A big rattle, a foam-filled fabric cube with a bell inside (stitch on a piece of strap or ribbon to dangle it by), or this Super Kicker. It's big, it swings, it makes sounds. Dangle it by the yarn handle.

SUPER KICKER

Ideal Intro Age: 4 Months
Age Range: 4 to 8 Months
FOR SUPERVISED PLAY ONLY

Tools & Materials

- Empty cereal or cracker box, with the lining (and crumbs) removed

- Piece of thick yarn or ribbon, about 24″ long

- Scissors, knife, or large nail (for punching holes)

- Jingle bells, small rattles, dried beans, or other small soundmakers

- Tape

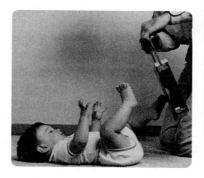

A great toy for spirited kicking fun—the homemade Super Kicker.

Directions

1. Drop the soundmakers into the clean, empty box.
2. Punch a hole in each narrow side, near the top.
3. Thread the yarn or ribbon through both holes and tie the ends together to form a loop.
4. Tape the lid securely shut.

SAFETY NOTE: For supervised play only. If left alone, your baby might try to pick off—and eat—the tape. Also, if she should get the box open, she might try to swallow the soundmakers.

At 3 or 4 months old, babies enjoy being pulled up to a sitting position.

BEGINNING TO SIT

Babies go through several stages in learning to sit up. At about 3 or 4 months, when they easily control the muscles supporting the head, most babies enjoy sitting while supported in a parent's lap or in a swing or other seat. They also enjoy being pulled to the sitting position, in junior versions of sit-ups.

- Lay your baby on her back on a smooth surface (the crib mattress, your bed, your lap, etc.).

- Grasp her hands and s-l-o-w-l-y pull her to the sitting position. Hold tight so she doesn't fall.

- Gently lower her again.

At first her back may sag and her head may lag behind her shoulders. But as her muscles strengthen she sags less and less. In fact, between about 5 and 6 months she might grab your extended hands and pull *herself* up.

Around 6 months most babies can sit with minimal support—perhaps with a small pillow behind the back or with just one hand held to aid their balance. When sitting, too, a baby might lean forward and support her weight on her outstretched arms. Within a month or so most babies sit fully upright.

More ways to help:

○ When your baby begins sitting alone, let her practice on a soft surface or surround her with pillows. These cushion her temporary tumbles and reduce discouragement.

○ Once she's up, the novice sitter might not be able to get out of the sitting position without help. A slumping back or an unhappy face might tell you that she's ready to return to lying on her stomach or back, or wants you to pick her up.

TOYS & GAMES FOR THE CRAWLER

Crawling is a giant stride toward independence. Once your baby begins scooting around under her own power, usually between 8 and 10 months, she need no longer depend totally on others to choose her play spaces and materials. She helps decide where she wants to go and what she wants to explore. Freedom! But with it comes responsibility—your responsibility for making the home safe for her excursions.

SAFETY NOTE: Now that your baby is crawling it's time to babyproof your home. Check out the suggestions in a good child care, child development, or specialized safety book.

Your baby has been preparing for crawling all this year; you've helped with massages, exercises, all types of general large-muscle play. Now that she seems ready for this new milestone, give her some extra practice. Make sure she has plenty of chances to flail about stomach-down on a firm surface. Placing your hands against the soles of her feet, so she has something to push against, might give her the traction she needs to get started.

Add encouragement on the front end, too. For instance, offer a favorite toy or delectable finger food for her to crawl to and capture. Or invite her to crawl into your outstretched arms.

Once your baby starts crawling fairly well, she needs no encouragement other than the thrill of moving about under her own power. (In truth, at times you'll wish that she weren't so self-driving!) But after mastering the rudiments, she probably likes the additional challenge of these games and toys.

Keep in mind that babies move forward in many different ways—rolling, creeping, pulling themselves along with their hands while sitting, slithering like a snake. Not all babies use the conventional hands-and-knees method of crawling.

Simple Games

○ Drag a pull toy slowly across the floor for your baby to pursue. Make sure she catches it after a time. Is she getting pretty speedy? Pull it faster.

○ Roll a ball and invite her to "Go get it."

○ Get down on the floor yourself and let her chase you. "Ah—ya got me!"

Interestingly, your baby probably won't flee if you reverse roles and try to chase her. Most children don't understand the role of the pursued until about 18 months of age. According to play specialist Dr. Brian Sutton-Smith:

It seems that when we learn how to behave socially, we first learn just one side of the relationship. Later we learn the other side. Then still later we put them both together. So here children learn the social relationship of chasing and escaping, first by chasing, next by escaping, then with both together.

Floor Pillows

Big, soft pillows are wonderful for active play like pounding on or crawling over, or quiet times like nestling into for a brief rest or sharing a picture book with you. Let your baby play on the floor with your bed pillows. Or make her a T-shirt Pillow of her very own. If you have time, make several; different sizes can have different functions. Your baby can flop on or roll or crawl over a large pillow on the floor. A group of medium-sized pillows double as soft building boulders. Your older toddler might also use them in a gentle pillow fight (the sleeves are easy hand-holds). Still smaller pillows can be tossed and caught. Pillows with fetching patterns make unique room decorations.

T-SHIRT PILLOWS

Ideal Intro Age: 9 Months
Age Range: 9 to 36 Months

Tools & Materials

- T-shirt with a smashing colorful design

- Stuffing material: polyester fiberfill or shredded foam; make sure it's machine washable and dryer safe

- Sewing machine or needle and thread

A homemade T-shirt Pillow is terrific for crawling over, nestling into for a rest.

Directions

1. Sew closed the sleeve holes and neck.
2. Stuff the shirt tightly through the open bottom and sew closed.

HINT: For a deluxe (albeit more time-consuming) version, sew patches of different textured fabrics onto the T-shirt before stuffing. Your baby likes exploring these varied surfaces. Make sure all the patches are securely attached and the fabrics are machine washable.

Tunnels for Crawling Through

Tunnels are mysterious and exciting. For your baby, crawling through a tunnel is a form of Peekaboo—she disappears, then reappears like magic. The tunnel itself is a cozy sort of temporary hideout. Older babies and toddlers like having their own turf in the larger adult environment.

Any piece of furniture under which she fits can be a tunnel, be it coffee table or dining room chair. Or, you can make a tunnel from a large cardboard carton. Tape shut the top flaps and cut tunnel-shaped openings in any two opposing sides. Make sure you leave some "framing" around the tunnel openings—these give the box stability. Or make the soft textured Fuzzy Crawl-through below.

TUNNEL GAMES

- Put a toy at one end of the tunnel for your baby to crawl toward and retrieve.

- Play Follow the Leader: You crawl through the tunnel first (if you can fit), your baby follows. Or an older sibling can lead your baby.

- A tunnel can be part of the Indoor Obstacle Course, page 96.

The homemade Fuzzy Crawl-through adds delightful texture to all-fours trips.

FUZZY CRAWL-THROUGH

Ideal Intro Age: 10 Months
Age Range: 10 to 24 Months

Tools & Materials

○ Carpet remnant, about 6′ × 3′; it must have a fairly stiff backing

○ Strong tape—carpet, duct, or reinforced wrapping tape

Directions

1. Roll the carpet length-wise into a cylinder, with the backing side out.
2. Secure with two or three bands of tape stretched around the circumference of the rolled carpet.

HINT: You might also try a tunnel with a different diameter. Remember that the diameter of a circle is roughly one-third of its circumference (distance around). Thus, a six-foot piece of carpet, when rolled, creates a tunnel about two feet in diameter.

PLAY TIPS

○ For a different sort of exercise, lay your baby across the outside of this carpet tunnel, hold her firmly by the waist or thighs, and gently roll her back and forth.

○ Stand this tunnel on end—it makes a great place to store balls and large toys. An older toddler might also like using it as a giant container for tossing balls and stuffed toys into. Then she can push it over—*crash! yay!*—to get them again.

Obstacle Course

Combine several things to crawl over, under, around, and through into a baby-sized obstacle course.

INDOOR OBSTACLE COURSE

Ideal Intro Age: 10 Months
Age Range: 10 to 18 Months

Tools & Materials

- Simple obstacles for baby to crawl over, under, around, and through. Some suggestions:

  - Large T-shirt Pillow, page 93
  - Fuzzy Crawl-through, page 95
  - Firm chair or sofa cushions
  - Plain cardboard boxes
  - Dining room chair (without stretchers near the floor), for crawling under
  - Giant stuffed animals

Directions

1. Scatter some obstacles around the floor.
2. Encourage your baby to crawl from one to another, following a "course." Over this pillow. Around this box. Under this chair. Through this tunnel. Big hugs and applause for completing maneuvers!

Play Tips

- Try some Follow the Leader! You lead the way around the course, your baby follows. This game is usually a favorite for an older brother or sister to play with baby, because she so admires their sophisticated ways.

○ Chase the Toy: This time a favorite toy leads the way. You shake it beside each obstacle, your baby scoots around trying to catch it. Be sure to give her the prize if she seems to be getting frustrated by the elusive chase.

UP WE GO

Soon after your baby learns to crawl she begins climbing. Now she's magically drawn to the staircase. Remember: It's unsafe! The padded steps of Climb & Slide are better. They also form the base for a first sliding board.

CLIMB & SLIDE

Ideal Intro Age: 12 Months
Age Range: 12 to 18 Months
FOR SUPERVISED PLAY ONLY

Build this homemade Climb & Slide to challenge the crawler; cover it with a large sheet of cardboard to make a first sliding board.

Tools & Materials

- Several firm couch or chair seat cushions
- Large cardboard box

Directions

1. For Climbing: Build a series of broad steps with the cushions.
2. For Sliding: Cut open the cardboard box to make a long runway. Be sure there are no staples or rough edges! Lay it on top of the cushion steps.

SAFETY NOTE: Because your crawler is so keen to climb, it's time to put a safety gate across the home staircase. Block both the top and the bottom. Put a gate at the top of the basement steps, too.

Play Tips

- For Climbing: Your toddler starts at the bottom of the steps, you're at the top. Encourage her to crawl up and get the prize (a toy, a big hug). Make sure she doesn't tumble off the side.

- For Sliding: Initially, it's best if both parents take part. One stands at the top and holds the cardboard from sliding forward. The other holds your toddler by waist or legs and helps her slide down to the bottom. When she sits quite confidently and slides well, let her try it without being held.

FIRST STEPS

Now the truly big achievement—walking. Even before your baby takes those all-important first steps, usually between 10 and 15 months, she's been pulling herself to a standing position by holding a support, like the crib or playpen rail, or the sofa. For walking practice she probably cruises from one end of the sofa to the other, moving hand-over-hand, or around the coffee table (be sure it hasn't a sharp edge). These trial excursions strengthen her legs and help her learn to balance while standing. Help, too, by walking with her, holding one or both of her hands.

Does she seem ready to join the upright race? Stand her on the floor. When she's steady on her feet, let go, back up a few steps, and call to her with outstretched arms. "Come on, Alexis, come to Daddy. Good for you, Alexis!"

Like crawling, walking is its own reward. Yet also like crawling, there are games and toys that make it more fun.

○ Both parents sit a few feet apart on the floor. Send your toddler back and forth, like a go-between. She might carry a "present" (a toy) from parent to parent. Reward her crossings with thanks and hugs.

The new walker loves being a go-between from parent to parent.

○ Take frequent strolls outside. The terrain of hard flat sidewalk and gently rolling lawn is quite different from floor and carpet.

○ Try more games of chase. You hobble away on hands and knees, your toddler pursues on two legs. Make sure she catches you.

○ Since the skilled walker often likes to carry something, invite her to be your special messenger. She might bring you something (unbreakable!) from the coffee table or bookshelf, or help you carry the laundry, or tote a single item (box of cereal) in from the car after a shopping trip.

Pull & Push Toys

The experienced walker also likes dragging a pull toy about as she strolls. The best ones make sounds so that your child is sure the toy is still following her without having to turn around to look. A pull toy with parts that can be shaken, rolled, and fitted or stacked onto the base offers many added play opportunities.

Starting at around 18 months or so, toddlers also like push toys with rigid handles. These, too, are more fun if they make sounds and spin or otherwise move as your child pushes them. Current favorites include plastic lawn mowers, shopping carts, and vacuum cleaners, since these have built-in imitation appeal.

RAMP GAMES

If your toddler loves balls and toys that roll (and most toddlers do), add novelty to her play with some ramp games. They're fun ways to practice eye-hand and locomotion skills.

○ Simplest: You roll a toy down the ramp. It races across the floor, and your toddler chases after it (crawling, creeping, toddling, whatever) and brings it back to you.

○ Your toddler rolls the toy down the ramp; you chase it.

○ Each of you holds a rolling toy on the top of the ramp. Ready—set—*go!* Release your toys. Down they zip . . . across the floor they zoom. Whose went fastest? Farthest? Good game for siblings! For variety, see who can retrieve her toy and bring it back to the top of the ramp first.

○ You let go of the toy, your toddler tries to catch it at the bottom of the ramp. (Best if you use a long, sloping ramp.)

○ Ramp Bowling: Set up pins at the bottom for your toddler to knock over with her rolling toy. Try plastic tumblers, tall wooden blocks, tennis ball cans, empty plastic bottles.

SAFETY NOTE: You should supervise these games, because left alone your toddler might try to walk up or slide down the ramp. Most of these homemade versions won't support her weight.

First, though, you need to create a ramp.

Ramps add drama, excitement, lots of skill-building exercise; check out the Ramp Games.

RAMPS FOR ROLLER GAMES

Ideal Intro Age: 15 Months
Age Range: 12 to 36 Months
FOR SUPERVISED PLAY ONLY

Tools & Materials

- RAMP—any broad plank that's at least 12″ long (longer, if possible) and about 9″ to 12″ wide:

  - Extra shelf from the bookcase

  - Large cutting board or kitchen "counter saver"

  - Long, flat gift box

  - Spare piece of lumber or plank bought at a lumberyard or home repair store; make sure it has no splinters or sharp edges!

- SUPPORT:

  - Couch cushions

  - Stack of books

  - Cardboard box

  - Postal Box Block, page 72

Directions

Rest one end of the ramp on the support.

KEEP IN MIND: The shorter the ramp and higher the support, the faster the toy rolls.

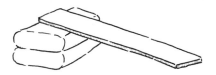

TERRIFIC TUBES

Large mailing tubes and rolling toys small enough to fit inside create dramatic play possibilities for the toddler 15 months and older. You can buy tubes at the stationery or office supply store. Cut off both ends. Tennis balls are great for these games. So are transparent balls with spinners inside.

○ You drop the ball into the tube, your toddler chases it when it emerges.

○ You hold the tube, your toddler drops the ball inside and chases it.

○ You hold one end of the tube, your toddler holds the other. Put a ball into the tube and roll it back and forth by tilting the tube one way, then the other.

○ When your toddler plays alone: Tape or tie a tube to the outside of the stair banister, slanting down and low enough for your toddler to reach easily. For a change of game, sit a basket on the floor under the tube to catch the balls.

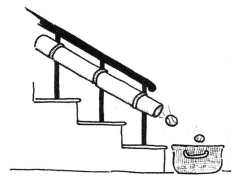

HINT: Cardboard tubes, all sizes, are fun even without the rolling toys. Peek at each other through a short tube (from an empty roll of paper towels, perhaps?). Or whisper to each other. Longer, stronger tubes are fine toddler baseball bats. Your child will find plenty of other uses, too.

SAFETY NOTE: A reminder . . . Ping-Pong balls are too small! Your toddler might get one lodged in her throat.

A temporary toddler-sized balance beam—for a more permanent version, see the homemade Balance Bridge.

BRIDGES & BALANCE BEAMS

Another challenge for the steady walker is a low bridge to walk across. This is often called a balance beam, although on a real one the surface is narrow; for this age it must be wide. You can make a temporary version by resting a broad plank on two boxes, or even on the stretchers between the legs of two chairs. Always supervise, though, because the plank might easily shift around. Also, hold your toddler's hand for early crossings.

NOTE: Some toddlers hesitate walking a balance beam, others take to it immediately. If your child balks, it's better not to force her.

This homemade Balance Bridge is a more permanent version. And when your child is older, it will probably inspire all sorts of fantasy play (the drawbridge over a castle moat, the bridge in the *Three Billy Goats Gruff*).

○ **BALANCE BRIDGE**

Ideal Intro Age: 15 Months
Age Range: 15 to 36 Months

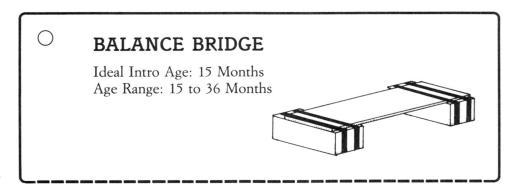

Tools & Materials

- ○ Wooden plank or shelf, about 12″ wide and 24″ to 36″ long

- ○ 2 cardboard boxes, at least 12″ long and wide, and about 6″ high

- ○ Newspaper

- ○ Strong packing or wrapping tape

Directions

1. Stuff each box completely full with wadded newspaper and tape closed. The paper adds strength.
2. Tape a box on each end of the plank. Use two bands of tape per box, and run each band across the plank and all the way around the box, as shown.

RIDING TOYS

Most parents I've interviewed introduce a riding toy when their child is just about 12 months old. This seems to be a good age, as long as you're aware of just how the new toddler uses it.

From 12 to about 15 months, toddlers don't ride a toy in the conventional sense. Rather, they get on and off. And on and off. They use it as a perch from which to observe their surroundings. They sit on it and push *backwards*. They get off and push it across the floor. They sit on it.

From about 15 months on toddlers begin pushing themselves forwards on a riding toy. They also turn it upside down and play with the wheels. At these young ages, a toddler usually isn't able to steer it accurately or use pedals. But she does like to be pushed.

Steering usually comes in between 18 and 24 months, pedaling a bit later. So we can say there are two phases of riding toys, with an appropriate type for each:

- 12 to 18 months, when ride-ons should be simple, nonpedal, and nonsteerable (although if the toy does have steering, it isn't automatically a drawback—just not a necessity).

- 18 months on up, when toys should offer steering and pedaling, even though these features (especially the pedals) might get little play for the first few months.

When Choosing a Ride-on

You'll find a staggering array of riding toys on the market. The following guidelines, taken from a survey of parents and teachers, might help you choose the best for your child. No one toy will have all these features, so decide which you think are most important. Also, take your toddler with you when making your selection, to ensure that she can handle the particular toy; that is, get on and off unaided, manage the steering, and so forth.

FAVORITE RIDE-ON FEATURES

- Easy mount/dismount. Make sure your toddler can get on and off all by herself. Otherwise she'll cry for your help—and you won't always be able to comply. Also keep in mind that younger toddlers tend to "walk into" a riding toy from the back. They can't swing their leg over the seat.

- Covered storage compartment that you can easily clean. All kinds of things—dirt, twigs, food—will find their way inside.

- A contoured seat that cradles your toddler, so that she doesn't slide off backwards. However, be sure that the backrest isn't so high that it hampers her ability to get on and off.

- A horn, bell, or other soundmaker that she can activate.

- Concealed wheels, or a wheelbase that's long enough so your toddler doesn't bump the front wheels with her toes. Remember—at first she pushes herself backwards.

○ Stability when turned upside down. This is a favorite way toddlers play with their ride-ons.

○ Additional activities, like a telephone, toys to fit onto the ride-on, a workbench, or the like.

○ Stability. A ride-on shouldn't easily tip forward, backwards, or sideways. To test a steering toy, turn the wheels all the way to one side and give a tug forward. If it tips readily, look for one with better balance.

○ For you: A ride-on should be compact enough for easy storage, light enough to carry from indoors to outdoors or from room to room, and easy to wash.

JUMPING AND BOUNCING FUN

"Stop bouncing on the bed!" thundered Daddy from downstairs as the chandelier swung madly over the dining room table.

"You'll break it—or your neck," Mummy called up the staircase in chorus.

Remember way back when? Well, with this Toddler Trampoline, your young child can jump, roll, flop, and flounder to heart's content—sparing furniture from destruction. It's best for homes with plenty of toddler playspace, since it takes up a lot of room.

This homemade Toddler Trampoline was a hit in schools; you can make your own.

○ 107 ○

○

TODDLER TRAMPOLINE

Ideal Intro Age: 18 Months
Age Range: 15 to 36 Months

Tools & Materials

- ○ Single bed mattress (or even the crib mattress)

- ○ Fitted sheet

Directions

Put the sheet on the mattress, the mattress on the floor.

HINTS: Since this mattress is for active play rather than sleeping, its condition doesn't matter as long as the cover isn't ripped. Look for a used mattress in the want ads, or at garage and yard sales. Also, if space is a problem, you can store this trampoline under a bed during non-playtimes.

SAFETY NOTE: Although most toddlers can't really bounce like circus tumblers, it's safest to position this trampoline a few feet from any wall when your child uses it unsupervised.

Play Tips

- ○ Initially your toddler will probably like just walking around on her Toddler Trampoline—it's not firm like the floor or yard. She'll gradually work up to falling and flopping and jumping. Jumping is especially fun when you hold her hands, or hold her under her arms and bounce her up and down.

- ○ Put some lively music on the radio or stereo.

TODDLER BALL GAMES

As a single item, a ball is probably the most indispensable toy for active play. It can be rolled, bounced, thrown, caught, kicked, whacked with a stick, dropped through a hoop, chased after—and that's just the beginning. Collect a variety of balls for your toddler. Different balls lend themselves to different types of play, depending on their size and material. And different children play with balls different ways, depending on the *child's* size and interests. Here are some games and ideas to get you started.

○ Sit a few feet apart on the floor and roll a ball back and forth. Your toddler's aim might be a bit off, but she'll have fun trying, and fun exchanging this object between you.

○ Safe Throwing: Use a rolled-up pair of socks as a ball. Ask your toddler to toss it to you. She'll probably throw it anywhere—even behind her—but the soft socks won't damage anything. With lots of practice she'll improve her aim.

○ Inflated beach balls are a special treat because they're so large (and therefore look "heavy" to a toddler), but are light enough for her to carry easily. Bounce a beach ball on her head. Roll it back and forth between you two (or three or more). Hold your toddler under her arms so she's standing, and swing her lightly back and forth so she "kicks" the ball.

○ Balloons, too, are magical balls. Sit facing each other and bat a balloon back and forth. Or demonstrate how batting a balloon by oneself keeps it aloft. Or drop a balloon for your toddler to catch. *For safety's sake,* always supervise her play with balloons. If one should pop, she might choke on the limp rubber. See also the Hand Paddles, page 115.

Balls inspire so many kinds of play; they're indispensable active toys.

○ Near 24 months, your toddler might be able to catch a ball tossed to her. Usually, she'll stretch out both arms, catch the ball between them, then cradle it and draw it to her chest. Ask her to try tossing it back.

○ At this age she can probably also kick a ball if you hold her hand for balance. Alone she might walk into the ball rather than kick it conventionally. True kicking is hard; it requires balancing on one foot while swinging the other.

○ A large rubber ball and several coffee cans or tennis ball cans make a nice clangy bowling set. Show how to roll the ball and knock the cans down. Then let your toddler try, with you playing pinboy. Don't be surprised if she devises her own way of playing. Some toddlers I know, rather than rolling the ball, carry it up to the cans and knock them over. Some toddlers toss the ball. Some carry the ball and kick the cans over.

Junior bowling!

To help insure success, create an alley that prevents the ball from straying off course. The sides can be made from couch cushions, cardboard boxes, or Postal Box Blocks, page 72. Or try outdoor bowling. The sidewalk is the alley, the grass on either side helps guide the ball.

ARM GAMES FOR OLDER TODDLERS

Pulling Punches

Is your toddler momentarily angry or frustrated? A few rounds at a punching bag can help work off some feistiness. It's better than her socking you or a sibling.

A punching bag fits into less pugnacious times, too. Hitting a hanging bag is a fine way for your toddler to exercise her arms and practice eye-hand coordination. (From her point of view, though, it's merely a fun way to play.) This indoor Punching Bag is perfect.

PUNCHING BAG

Ideal Intro Age: 18 Months
Age Range: 18 to 36 Months
BEST FOR SUPERVISED PLAY (see SAFETY NOTE below)

A homemade Punching Bag thrills any young pugilist.

Tools & Materials

- Old pair of adult-sized blue jeans (or other slacks)
- Newspaper, about 20 or more double-page sheets
- Needle and thread or sewing machine
- Piece of strong rope, about 5' long
- Hammer
- Large nail or hook

Directions

1. Cut off one leg from the jeans, turn this leg inside out, and sew closed the cut end.
2. Turn right-side-out again and stuff about three-fourths full with crumpled newspaper.
3. Tie closed the opening with one end of the rope. Make the knot *tight.*
4. Tie a small loop in the other end of the rope, and hang in the center of an open doorway, slipping the loop over a strong nail or sturdy hook driven into the door frame. The bottom of the bag should be a foot or two off the floor.

HINT: Save the remainder of the jeans for making the Blue Jeans Bag, page 182.

SAFETY NOTE: This is best for supervised play because on her own, your toddler may swing on the bag. One, it might come crashing down under her weight, which could be dangerous. Two, she might swing into the side of the door frame, injuring herself. Slip the bag off the nail when playtime's over. It's probably safer if your child doesn't play alone with this toy even when it's not hanging from a support. There's a slight chance that she might get tangled in the rope and choke.

Play Tips

○ Your beginning puncher might be more confident if you hold the bag still as she slugs it.

○ Add some early learning about numbers by counting aloud each time your toddler punches the bag.

○ Put some bouncy music on the radio or stereo to accompany your child's workout.

○ Hang the bag outside, from a low tree limb, and let your older toddler (over 24 months) swat it with a child-sized plastic baseball bat or plastic tennis racquet, or even a sturdy cardboard tube.

Tossing Game

Here's another standby from our own childhood—tossing a ball, bean-bag, or other object at a target. Is this the forerunner of basketball? Major league pitching? Carnival games where tossing a baseball brings down a pyramid of milk bottles? Who knows? But those and other adult pastimes call for a keen eye and fine aim, skills that this game certainly develops.

Keep in mind that tossing at a target isn't as simple as you might think. First, your toddler has to understand the point of the game—hitting the target with the tossed toy. Second, she must have the ability to let go of the toy at will, and the coordination to aim her throws. These are developed with time and practice. So in the early stages, your child might stand right by the target and just drop the ammo into the box, or hit the ammo against the target and then place it into the box. That's fine—this game has no real rules.

The Target Toss toy below gives ideas of good targets to create and appropriate ammunition.

TARGET TOSS

Ideal Intro Age: 24 Months
Age Range: 24 to 36 Months

Tools & Materials

- ○ Target:

    - ○ Large piece of paper or posterboard

    - ○ Crayons or felt-tipped markers

    - ○ Masking tape, at least 1″ wide

- ○ Basket or shallow box

- ○ Ammunition: Any things your toddler can toss easily:

○ Beanbags (see Sock Beanbags, page 63)

○ Small stuffed animals

○ Wiffle balls

○ Plastic blocks

Directions

1. Draw a colorful target on the paper or posterboard. Some suggestions:

   ○ Silly animal face with huge open mouth

   ○ Pair of outstretched hands

   ○ Bull's-eye of different colored rings

   ○ Goofy clown

2. Tape this onto a wall and set the box or basket underneath to catch the tossed ammo (and store it between playtimes).

Play Tips

○ Count each object as your toddler tosses it—good for early number learning.

○ Take turns tossing at the target. Your older child might like to play, too.

○ If the target is an animal face with gaping jaws, you can pretend that the ammo is food, and you and she are tossing tidbits to the hungry beast. Beanbags, with their amorphous shape, are good for this version. "And here's another fish for Stella Seal."

○ If the target is a clown or other face, pretend he's a bad actor and you're pelting him with rotten tomatoes. "Boo! Hiss!"

Handball Games

Many older toddlers like to swat balls and balloons with their hands—sort of a junior version of handball. The trouble is, they sometimes lack the coordination to hit accurately. Because a homemade Hand Paddle "makes" your child's hand much larger, it helps insure success.

HAND PADDLES

Ideal Intro Age: 24 Months
Age Range: 24 to 36 Months

Toss a wadded newspaper ball for your toddler to smack with her homemade Hand Paddle.

Tools & Materials

○ Paper plate, dinner-sized; choose the rigid molded type with the rim (Chinet); an ordinary paper plate is too flimsy

○ Elastic strap, 1″ wide and about 10″ long

○ Knife

○ Needle and thread

Directions

1. Make two slits, about five inches apart, in the plate. Each should be a little more than one inch long.
2. Thread the elastic strap through both slits, then sew the strap ends together, pulling up any slack in the elastic.
3. To wear the paddle, slip a hand between the strap and the bottom of the plate.

FRONT   BACK

PLAY TIPS

○ Give your toddler a Hand Paddle and a balloon. How many times can she bat the balloon into the air without letting it touch the ground? (Count each hit aloud, too, for number learning.)

○ You and your toddler (or your toddler and a sibling) each wear a paddle and hit the balloon back and forth.

○ Crumple a sheet of newspaper into a ball, then run cellophane or masking tape around the outside to hold its shape. You pitch this ball, your toddler smacks it with her Hand Paddle. Or use a plastic wiffle ball, or even a large foam "Nerf" ball.

○ Create a newspaper ball, tape on a piece of twine, and hang it outdoors from a clothesline, low branch, or other support. Your toddler can swat it like a tetherball. You can also hang a plastic wiffle ball.

SAFETY NOTE: Supervise your toddler's play with a balloon. It could frighten her if it pops. And if she put the limp rubber into her mouth she might choke on it.

WATER SLIDE

A slippery, slidy sheet of wet plastic on the lawn is the perfect cooler on those sweltering summer days—for your toddler, her friends and older siblings, even you if you want to join the fun. This Slippery Slider is not only delightful, it's great exercise to boot.

SLIPPERY SLIDER

Ideal Intro Age: 24 Months
Age Range: 18 to 36 Months
FOR SUPERVISED PLAY ONLY

Beat the heat with a homemade Slippery Slider.

Tools & Materials

○ *Heavy-gauge* plastic tarpaulin or painting dropcloth. (Thin plastic dropcloths will *not* stand up to the vigorous play this toy gets. Also, thin plastic might suffocate a child if misused.) Heavy plastic tarpaulins are usually available at hardware stores, home supply centers, large discount department stores, some paint stores, and camping supply centers.

○ Lawn sprinkler.

Directions

1. Spread the tarpaulin flat over a patch of lawn—*not* a bare spot of ground (it'll get muddy), and *not* a driveway or other hard surface.

2. Position the sprinkler near one end of the tarpaulin and turn on the water. When the tarp's completely wet, start playing!

HINTS: Keep the water running as long as you play. Also, move this slide around occasionally so that the grass underneath doesn't smother, or become too waterlogged, or get cooked by the hot sun coming through the plastic.

SAFETY NOTE: *Always* supervise a young child when she's in or around water. There's ever a chance of drowning—and the younger she is, the worse the chance. Even with the Slippery Slider, she could possibly inhale some water.

Play Tips

o Play speedboat: Grab your toddler's ankles and push her around the wet surface of the Slippery Slider while she lies on her stomach.

o Play "the old man and the sea." You're the fisherman, your toddler is the prize fish. She grabs the end of a rope while lying on her stomach, you pull her around the slider.

o Does your child enjoy fantasy play? Ask her to pretend she's a whale . . . a goldfish . . . a sea horse. . . . Or you both can pretend you're sea creatures and act out an underwater adventure.

o Great toy for older siblings to use, too. Make sure they don't become too rambunctious around your toddler.

TO SUM UP

Just think! In three short years your child has changed from a tiny curled-up newborn into a confident toddler who runs and jumps and climbs. But physical skill is only one part of her marvelous self. Let's look next at language.

LANGUAGE FUN

"W-a-a-a-a-a-a-h-h-h-h!"

"O-o-o-o-o-o-o-o-o-o."

"Babadabadadawawawababa."

"Ma ma!"

"Doggie!"

"Daddy car."

"Uh-oh, juice all gone."

Learning to talk, like any other skill, is a behavioral process that begins at birth and proceeds in a continuous pattern throughout the early years. Like other skills, too, language learning has several important milestones as illustrated in the utterances above: crying, cooing vowel sounds, babbling, first words, early sentences, and the like. These unfold according to each child's inner developmental timetable. You don't really teach your baby to talk, just as you don't teach him to sit up or walk. But there are lots of ways to enhance your child's language skills through play.

DEVELOPMENTAL OVERVIEW

Talking is such a complicated process that it would take thousands of pages to describe all the intricate steps. Keep that in mind as you read this drastically abbreviated overview of some important highlights. Also remember, that the ages given are averages. Almost no baby follows this pattern to a T. Also, since most research has been done with babies and mothers (rather than fathers), findings are usually given in terms of baby-mother pairs.

Birth to About 3 Months

At birth a baby is primed for communication. He prefers human speech (especially his mother's voice) to any other sounds, and listens to speech in a special way. Within a few weeks a baby and mother develop a sort of prototype conversation. As the mother speaks, the baby moves his face, lips and tongue, arms and hands, and even whole body in a kind of synchrony. For example, when the mother pauses, the baby moves as if it's his turn to "speak."

From a very young age a baby can tell the difference between similar

All experts agree that talking to your baby is the absolute best way to build language skills.

speech sounds, for instance, *pa* and *ba.* Recognizing such differences is the foundation of understanding any language.

The newborn's first "word" is his cry, and over the early weeks cries form a symbolic language. Some say "I'm hungry." Some say "I'm bored." Some call urgently with an "I need you!" intensity. Parents pick up these differences almost instinctively. When you respond to cries you are teaching your baby something else about language—that his vocalizations engage another person. This is another early form of conversation.

By about 6 weeks a baby conveys feelings with sounds other than cries. And by 3 months he coos and gurgles and squeals with pleasure.

3 to About 6 Months

A baby this age experiments with making various sounds. He chuckles and laughs, gurgles and squeals, growls, grunts, and blows bubbles with saliva. He may vocalize tunefully or make long "speeches" when looking at people or things that interest him. By 6 months he usually makes both single and double syllables—for example, *ka, muh, adah, erleh.*

His language comprehension is likewise growing. In familiar mother-baby games he may make appropriate gestures to key words, such as trying to clap his hands as you recite Pat-a-cake. Or when you accompany certain words in a familiar rhyme with tickling, he may begin to laugh just at the words alone, anticipating the tickle.

6 to About 9 Months

A baby this age can discriminate different harmonic patterns in the way sentences are uttered. Questions have rising tunes, statements have falling tunes. Exclamations, like "What a shock you gave me!" have a different tune altogether. He also understands simple commands like "No, no" and "Bye-bye," and responds when called by name. He uses easily understood gestures as well to make his feelings known, such as waving away unwanted food or shaking his head when he doesn't want to do something.

The sounds he makes are becoming more like true speech. At first he makes consonant-vowel sounds like *ma, pa, da, di, wa,* which use primarily the lips. At first he makes such sounds one at a time, but soon he strings them into rhythmic babbles—*babababababababa*. Later he adds more difficult sounds: *s, f,* and *ts* (as in *cats*), although, interestingly, these rarely show up in first words. He uses his voice to make his feelings known and to get things he wants. He shouts for attention, or tries to make contact with another person with a cough or other noise. In a sense, we can say he vocalizes deliberately as a means of interpersonal communication.

9 to About 12 Months

Babbling peaks during this age. Babies make long, tuneful utterances that sound very much like real sentences if you don't listen too closely. They make different sounds to indicate different wants and needs. These can usually be interpreted correctly by parents and other close caregivers, but may mystify casual acquaintances. Near the end of this period (usually between 10 and 13 months), a baby says his first word that is generally understandable to almost everyone.

But way before this time, your baby understands many things said to him. Word comprehension always precedes and outpaces word produc-

Most babies say their first real word between 10 and about 13 months.

tion. At this age he knows his own name and the names of other familiar people. He understands and acts on simple commands, like "Come here" and "Show me your nose" and "Give the baby doll a kiss." He also indicates that he understands questions like "Do you want your bottle?" In fact, there's no real way to measure how much a baby does understand, but it easily surpasses his ability to say words.

12 to About 18 Months

Comprehension continues to outpace production. It's estimated that a child comprehends about fifty different words by 12 months of age; yet he usually doesn't say that many until 18 or 20 months.

A toddler this age points to familiar persons, animals, and objects when requested. He shows his own shoe or even a doll's shoe. He throws a ball when asked. In fact, he has many ways to demonstrate how much he understands.

After a child says his first words, his spoken vocabulary tends to grow one word at a time. Word rates vary, but most children have a vocabulary of thirty to fifty or more words by 18 months. He definitely delights in this new skill. He demands objects by pointing and vocalizing single words. He often names things and people just for the sheer pleasure of pronouncing the words and attaching them to the appropriate objects. When someone talks to him, he might echo prominent words or the last word in the sentence. He usually mispronounces words, because he lacks the muscular structure to formulate difficult word sounds, but even so most words are understandable to family members.

18 to 36 Months

During this period a toddler's vocabulary grows very rapidly. In one large study the 24-month-olds had an average speaking vocabulary of 200 words. But that was the *average;* the range was from 30 to over 400 words, more evidence that each child develops at his own pace. By three years, a child has a speaking vocabulary of several hundred words. Not surprisingly, these words are the most common and important. Even though the English language has over 400,000 words, about 500 words are used most often; in fact, they make up about 90 percent of typical adult conversations. A two-year-old has mastered nearly half of these 500 words, and the three-year-old almost all of them.

The other major development during this age span is putting words together to form sentences. Before 18 or 24 months, a child usually speaks in one-word utterances. Now he combines them, which greatly increases his ability to express himself. For instance, up to this point he might have said "more" or "cookie" to let you know he wanted another cookie. But since he spoke only one word, you couldn't be absolutely sure what he intended. What does he want more of? Or, what is he trying to say about a cookie? Now that he can say "More cookie" there's no questioning his intention! These phrases almost always reflect correct syntax, with proper subject-verb or verb-object order. For example, a toddler probably would not say "Cookie more."

After 24 months a child begins using longer and longer phrases so that by 30 months he really talks in sentences of three or more words.

COMMON QUESTIONS

Naturally, language growth doesn't proceed without hidden mysteries or apparent mistakes. Here are some of the topics that concern many parents I know.

How Do First Words Appear?

First words apparently grow out of babbling, although no one can state exactly how. Babbling is a universal language; babies around the world babble the same rich assortment of sounds, from the softer slurs of the Romance languages to the clicking sounds of some African dialects. It seems that babies continue to use the word sounds that are reinforced in their own language, and discard the others.

The process of turning babbles into words appears to involve three conditions:

1. A baby's physical ability to make particular sounds.
2. A baby's inborn interest in imitating words and word sounds he hears frequently.
3. Parents' encouragement to repeat sounds and turn them into words.

For an example, let's look at the word *da da*. It's a common first word, probably because:

1. The *da* sound is easy for a baby to make.
2. Parents often talk about a father, usually calling him Daddy.
3. Whenever a baby says *da da* even by accident, ecstatic parents usually encourage repeats. "He said 'da da'! He knows me! Say 'da da' again." When the baby, delighted with this new power, complies, parents again react enthusiastically, so he tries again. Over time, with parents' encouragement and gentle correction, *da da* becomes *Daddy*. Other common words, like *Mama, bay-bee, car,* and *doggie* probably evolve much the same way.

Why These Particular Words?

Even though every toddler hears and comprehends hundreds if not thousands of words, most toddlers have a very similar early speaking vocabulary. It's obvious why words like Mommy and Daddy appear in almost every early vocabulary. And it's obvious that most early words are things a toddler can pronounce or at least approximate easily. But that could be thousands of things. Why is *car* a favorite word, but not *coat?*

A baby's first words are almost always the names or labels of things he finds important or interesting. Language specialist Katherine Nelson studied the early vocabularies of 18 children, identifying the first 50 different words that each child spoke. She classified these words into six categories by type of word:

○ General name (*ball, car, cookie*)

○ Specific name (*Mommie, Daddy, Bowser*)

○ Action word *(look, bye-bye, give)*

○ Modifier *(mine, big)*

○ Personal-social *(please, no)*

○ Function *(what, where)*

She found that *65 percent* of all the words these children spoke were either general nouns or specific names. Similar studies have produced like findings.

When you examine the nouns more closely, other interesting patterns emerge. For example, of the words for toys, *ball* was by far the most popular, appearing nearly twice as often as *blocks* and three times as often as *doll.* Of furniture words, *clock* was three times as popular as such familiar baby items as *crib.* In the clothing category, *shoe* was ten times more common than *shirt* or *dress,* five times more common than *coat.* Yet in real life all are about as familiar. And in food words, *cookie, juice,* and *milk* easily led the list.

Other researchers have interpreted these lists and have speculated not only why these particular words are so popular, but why names of other objects just as familiar are omitted.

The conclusion is that toddlers first use names of objects that they can act on, or that move in interesting ways.

For example, *ball* is more popular than *block* or *doll* because it is far more active, and the toddler can do more with it. *Rattle,* which theoretically is a far more common toy, is not on the list at all. A *clock* makes interesting sounds and the hands move. *Crib,* certainly more familiar, is a static object and therefore rarely a favorite early word. A *car* is active, but a *tree* (which did not appear in any vocabulary) is just "there." *Shoe* beats *shirt*—each common, one as easy to pronounce as the other—because a toddler can take off his own shoes. Even favorite food words are those things—*juice, milk, cookie*—that the toddler easily feeds to himself. The toddler knows what a shirt and tree and coat and hundreds of other nouns are. It's just that, spontaneously, he's far less likely to include them in his early vocabulary of spoken words.

For fun, keep a list of your own toddler's growing vocabulary, and see how closely his first words match the types of words so popular in this study.

Is Bad Pronunciation a Problem?

For toddlers, mispronunciataion is the standard, not the exception. Most speech sounds, especially those involving complex coordination of the tongue, lips, and larynx, are difficult to make. Sounds like *sh, spa, spra, ch,* and *th,* for instance, are frequently mispronounced even by almost half of all 3-year-olds. Your toddler constantly substitutes a simpler sound for one more difficult: *dat* for *that, pitty* for *pretty, care* for *chair,* and the like.

Why Do Toddlers Mix Up Words?

A toddler often uses a single word to refer to several different objects. He might call every man *daddy.* Or call every round object *ball,* be it a stone, the moon, a radish, an orange. Or everything with four legs—pony, horse, pig, or cow—is a *doggie.* In other words, he refers to a variety of objects, actions, or people by the same name if they have one or more features in common.

Scientists call this *overextension.* When your toddler uses the same word for two objects, it can mean:

- He truly doesn't recognize the difference between two things; if he has never seen an orange before, he might really believe an orange *is* a ball.

- He doesn't know the name of one of them. If he's new to pigs, it's logical to believe that a pig is a type of dog.

- He doesn't know how to say the name of one object. He clearly knows that every man is not his daddy. Yet if he doesn't know the word *man,* he naturally substitutes the closest word he knows.

Your toddler loves to talk and to name things. Yet because his vocabulary lags behind his comprehension, he often lacks the correct word. So he does the best with what he knows. He overextends less as he learns new vocabulary words, and as he truly does learn the differences between seemingly similar objects.

GENERAL WAYS TO HELP

Talk to your baby! Even from the earliest months, even when you two aren't actively playing together, talk to your baby. He needs to hear the words and sounds of language in order to produce them himself. Talking also helps keep him in touch with you, from across the room or wherever you happen to be. It lets him know how special he is. When you're cooking dinner, tell him why you add certain spices to that pasta sauce, or why you knead the pastry dough. If you're cleaning up, tell him why you put the cups in that cupboard, the silverware in its special drawer. Or if you just need someone to spill your heart to, turn to your baby. You can be sure he won't gossip behind your back.

Keep in mind—this does not suggest that you turn into a chattering magpie. Too much talk, like almost anything in excess, is boring and dilutes its effect. But it does mean that talking to your baby is valuable—whatever his age.

When you and your young child play together, talk about his toys. Describe them as many ways as you can, repeating important words frequently and using plenty of adjectives. "See your ball, Joshua, your big, yellow ball? Look—it bounces. I'm going to roll the ball—can you catch it?" Encourage him to "talk" by asking questions and pausing for him to respond, even if only with a wave or a wiggle at early ages. Later he'll supply words, later still enter into more realistic conversations.

Be sure to name objects for him—things he's looking at as well as toys you're playing with together. He loves learning names of things well before he can say them himself. Name body parts at bath and changing time. As you undress him, a cheerful "Let's take off your shirt—lift up your arms," is much more educational and pleasant than undressing him

Draw your child's attention to new objects and events, and describe them as best you can.

in silence. Talk about the groceries as you shop, and again when you unpack at home. Take a tour of your house, stopping frequently to talk about all the things you and he see.

And always remember—talking should be light, easy, natural, and fun. If you start sounding too much like a language teacher, it loses spontaneity and enjoyment dwindles for both of you.

Also remember that it's probably best not to pressure your toddler too much as he's trying his new language skills. Admonishments to "Say *doggie* for your grandma, come on, say *doggie* for Grandma," when he's not in the mood, or insisting that he repeat a word until he pronounces it correctly, may discourage his attempts to talk. On the flipside, ecstatic enthusiasm at his *every* attempt to say a word is out of hand, too. Overabundant praise for an action not worthy of such accolades can overwhelm your toddler.

Some Specifics

○ When your young baby makes sounds, lean your face close to his and make the same sound right back. He'll probably smile—and may even make the sound again for your response.

○ When he begins to babble, babble right back and encourage him to babble right back to you. See how long you can keep the string of babbles going.

○ Once your baby begins saying words, encourage him to repeat the names of objects after you say them. "A nice red cup, all filled with juice. Here's your cup, Benjamin. Can you say *cup?*" At first he'll probably just say part of the word, like *ca,* or might mispronounce it as *dup.* That's fine—it's a good start. Encourage these attempts by modifying and expanding: "That's right, it's a *cup.* A red cup full of juice."

○ Gentle correction and expansion are the best ways to encourage your toddler as well. If he calls out "goggie" when your household canine races across the yard, you can respond with, "That's right, that's a doggie. He sure runs fast!" Or when he states "Daddy go" after his father leaves the house, you might say, "Yes, Daddy has gone to the store. What do you think he might buy?" This concluding question invites your toddler to continue the conversation if he likes.

○ You might need to act as occasional interpreter when your toddler talks to other people. Some of his pet words and idiosyncratic pronunciations will be incomprehensible to outsiders. Always let him try first, but step in when it's obvious that communication is failing.

○ At some point your toddler starts asking questions: "What dat?" "Who dat?" Sometimes it's questions, questions all day long. Most of these are legitimate requests for information, marking his fascination with learning names. However, sometimes these questions probably are merely a means for getting attention, as many parents have always suspected. Try to be patient, and answer him as best you can. But when you're preoccupied with other things, or are just too tired to respond to his inquiries, it's quite acceptable to tell him that you need a break.

PICTURES AND BOOKS

Books are the traditional way to enhance your baby's language skills. Hearing you read aloud helps him learn about the rhythms of language, grammar and sentence structure, and the sounds of words. Books build his vocabulary; they bring to him pictures of objects that he rarely encounters in his everyday life, such as baby animals. Reading together is a lovely emotional experience for you both, too.

I've found that babies usually go through typical stages in their interest in books.

○ Up to about 5 or so months, a baby usually likes looking quietly at pictures while listening to his parent talk about them. He rarely interacts physically with the book.

○ From 5 to about 9 months, a baby usually tries to handle a book as he does most objects: mouthing, pulling, twisting, and so forth. When he does concentrate on the book as a book, he might pat the pages and babble along as you talk about the pictures.

○ After 9 months, a baby shows increasing interest in books for their intended purpose. He looks at, pats, and points to pictures, tries to turn pages (often a few at a time if they're made of paper), and tries to say words.

○ During toddlerhood he shows increasing interest in books, first concentrating on the pictures. When he nears 2 years old, he enjoys plot and storyline as well.

Five- to nine-month-olds handle books like they do toys—roughly—so board or vinyl ones are best.

○ 131 ○

Pictures for Beginning Readers

For the first year or more you don't really read picture books to your baby. You talk about the pictures in ways you invent. So the first books can be pictures of any appropriate type, both in traditional books with pages or in less conventional formats. For instance, the Eye Targets, page 19, and Picture Parade, page 22, are both unconventional books. So are the following two homemade toys.

The room-decorating Picture Line is a picture "book" that's spread horizontally across the nursery wall. The clothespin-holder system lets you easily change the display whenever you come across a new picture your baby would like. To play, hold your baby close so he can see each picture as you talk about it.

Boxed Pictures is a three-dimensional "book" that's perfect for the baby who loves handling his reading materials; he can't rip the pages because there aren't any. To read: Talk about the pictures one by one, as you would with pictures in a book. To play: Your baby can drum on this cube with his hands, tumble it over like a ball, and (if you make several) build things with these colorful light blocks when he's older.

○

PICTURE LINE

Ideal Intro Age: 3 Months
Age Range: 3 to 12 Months

Tools & Materials

- ○ Long piece of clothesline
- ○ Several pinch-type clothespins
- ○ 2 hooks

This homemade Picture Line turns the nursery wall into an easily-changed picture "book."

Directions

1. Thread clothespins onto the clothesline.
2. Tie a loop in each end of the clothesline, and hang it up on hooks screwed into the wall. The line itself should be about level with your head.
3. From the clothespins, hang pictures that your baby might like. Choose those showing bright colors, familiar objects, animals, and faces. You can find lots of appropriate pictures in magazines. Or you can use pictures from a calendar, choose an appealing poster, or purchase reproductions of famous paintings at your local art museum. Maybe this will help your baby develop a lifelong interest in fine art.

HINT: When your baby becomes a toddler, turn this clothesline into the Wall-Line Scrapbook, page 172.

BOXED PICTURES

Ideal Intro Age: 6 Months
Age Range: 6 to 18 Months

Tools & Materials

○ Plain gift box with cover; use the square, boxy type (about 6″ or larger) rather than the long, flat type

Homemade Boxed Pictures are great for physical readers, since there are no pages to rip.

- Magazines or other sources of pictures
- Scissors
- White household glue

Directions

1. Glue the cover onto the box.
2. Cut appropriate pictures out of magazines. Remember, babies like faces, animals, and familiar objects (bottle, cup, pieces of clothing, toys, flower). Glue a picture on each face of the box. Make sure you glue completely around the very edge of each picture so that your baby can't pick it off.

Using Books

These suggestions mostly apply to picture books for babies and toddlers. The text, if any, is minimal and merely a springboard to get you going. Older toddlers also like storybooks with a plot and text you read word for word. Even so, you can continue to talk about the pictures as well.

- Point to and even tap on a pictured object as you talk about it. Trace your finger around its outline. Repeat its name in a variety of sentences. Describe it completely, using lots of adjectives. Make up a little story about it. Ask lots of questions, too—these involve your child. Invite him to trace or pat the object. When he's old enough to imitate sounds, ask him to join in vocally. For a long example:

  Well, look here, Paul, here's a puppy, a baby puppy. See the puppy? (Trace) She's such a funny puppy, a funny brown puppy. Look, she's wagging her long tail (point). Let's call her Barker, just like Aunt Helen's puppy. Look at Barker's

Encourage your toddler to point to pictured objects as you talk about them.

fuzzy brown ears—oh, look *(point),* her ears are pink inside. Do you see her ears? Can you show me the puppy's ears? That's right—fuzzy brown ears. And look at her tongue—a red tongue. Barker has a red tongue. *(Point)* I think this puppy is going to lick the little boy *(point)* with her tongue. She sure is. Barker is going to give the boy a kiss, a wet lickety kiss. Do you want a kiss, a puppy kiss? *(Comply)* Can you give me a puppy kiss, too? *(He does)* How nice. A nice wet puppy kiss. What does a puppy say? She says "Ruffff, ruffff." Barker says "Ruffff, ruffff." Can you sound like Barker? Can you sound like a puppy? Good!

Then if your baby is still interested in the puppy picture, talk about some other elements, or make up a brief tale about what the puppy might do next.

○ Sometimes your toddler points to an object unprompted. Follow his cues and expand. "Oh, yes, there's the baby bear, and all his friends are leaving. Is he waving bye-bye? I think he is. Can you wave bye-bye? Say 'Bye-bye' to friendly baby bear."

○ When looking at picture books of animals, make their funny noises. Ask your toddler to imitate you. When he knows his animal sounds by heart you can skip the demonstration. Point to any beast and ask "What does the ———— say?" You can also make the sounds of vehicles and invite imitation.

○ If the book has a recurring character, ask your toddler to find it on every page. "Can you find the gold bug in this picture?"

○ Always look to your child for cues. Is he getting bored? Go to the next picture. Does he want to linger? Pause as long as he likes. Is he fussy, does he strain against you? Maybe book time is over. Does your toddler bring you a book? It's time to start again.

Sometimes this, too, happens. Your toddler brings you a favorite volume, begging your attention. Fine. You put aside your cup of coffee and newspaper, get all cozy on the couch, open to page one, and then . . . shift, squirm, wiggle, he's struggling to get down and do something else. Fine. Seven minutes later, he's back with another book and that heart-melting look on his face. You put down the checkbook and pen and move to the couch. This session lasts for three pages before the fidgeting sets in. He's off again. Then five minutes later . . . Accede as long as your patience holds out, then promise that you'll read later, you're too busy now. And keep your promise.

○ And the most important suggestion of all—have fun! Be dramatic, and use different voices for different characters. Sing little songs or make up chants. Add sound effects—"Here's the little yellow cab, 's-c-r-e-e-e-c-c-h-h,' he goes around the corner, 'Beep beep,' he calls, 'Get out of my way.'" Your ebullience and infectious enjoyment bring a book to life.

In addition to the books you and your young child share together, he'll sometimes just like hearing you read aloud whatever *you* like to read—the newspaper, a magazine article, a novel or short story. The content doesn't matter to him; the warmth and security of your voice do. Reading aloud can even calm a fussy baby. And lying snugly, just listening to a bedtime story, certainly is a lovely way to drift into sleep.

Choosing Books for Babies and Young Toddlers

Each year hundreds of new baby-toddler books are printed, and since this is currently one of the fastest growing segments of the publishing field, you can expect an eye-popping array when you visit the bookstore or library. What are the favorite titles? Who knows! We once surveyed sixteen mothers and four teachers of babies from 2 to 12 months old, asking each to list the five books she and her baby (or her "pupils") liked most. The combined results included over 70 different titles! Much more interesting, though, are these features the favorite books share. They might help you choose the best books for *your* baby.

CONTENTS

- Clear, colorful, realistic pictures with uncluttered backgrounds.

- Action-oriented pictures rather than merely static objects to name.

- Pictures showing things that babies themselves typically do: eating, sleeping, playing with toys, taking a bath, playing peekaboo and other familiar games.

- Pictures showing clear and varied facial expressions, so that parents can talk about feelings and emotions.

- Pictures showing familiar objects, especially in use.

- Pictures of objects or activities that inspire sounds: animals (especially baby animals), vehicles, babies clapping their hands, and the like.

- Brief text or storyline, if any. However, rhymes, poems, chants, and songs are all popular.

PHYSICAL FEATURES

- Durability! Especially for books the baby and toddler handle. Cardboard books are the favorites, thick vinyl books second. Cloth books are *not* recommended; after they're washed they become as limp as dishrags.

- Smooth, rounded corners, especially on cardboard books.

- Washability. Favorite books get dirty.

- Textures and activities. In fact, the old standby *Pat the Bunny,* by Dorothy Kundhardt, is the only single book that emerged a favorite in our survey.

Choosing Books for Older Toddlers

Older toddlers also like stories with a plot—beginning, middle, and end. Again, there are hundreds of new titles yearly from which to choose. There are also some classics in the field, books that have been known and loved for years. In another survey, parents were given a list of about 60 acknowledged classics, and were asked to select the 10 they and their child liked best. Here some titles do stand out, as reported below. But even more importantly, the favorite books shared some specific themes. Keep these in mind as you shop.

- The story is simple and repetitive; this makes it easy for a toddler to follow. Suggested titles:

    Caps for Sale, by Esphyr Slobodkina

    Millions of Cats, by Wanda Gág

    Goodnight Moon, by Margaret Wise Brown

    The Little Engine That Could, by Watty Piper

    The Three Bears, by Paul Galdone

○ The text is full of rhythms and rhymes, including both poetry and silly rhyming words. Suggested titles:

Mother Goose

A Child's Garden of Verses, by Robert Louis Stevenson

When We Were Very Young, by A. A. Milne

Dr. Seuss books, the simplest ones

○ The story and pictures invite parent and child to play with sounds. Suggested titles:

The Train to Timbuctoo, by Margaret Wise Brown

The Little Engine That Could, by Watty Piper

The Three Bears, by Paul Galdone

Dr. Seuss books, the simplest ones

○ The main character has characteristics, behaviors, feelings, and emotions the toddler easily identifies with and understands. Suggested titles:

Corduroy, by Don Freeman

Where the Wild Things Are, by Maurice Sendak

The Tale of Peter Rabbit, by Beatrix Potter

Bedtime for Frances, by Russell Hoban

○ The storyline presents situations and routines the toddler himself often does; again, this helps him identify with the main character. Suggested titles:

Goodnight Moon, by Margaret Wise Brown

Bedtime for Frances, by Russell Hoban

Curious George, by H. A. Rey

○ 139 ○

○ The story has social-emotional lessons. For example, it presents strong family relationships, or has a powerful moral lesson, or shows a weak character overcoming adversity. Suggested titles:

Corduroy, by Don Freeman

The Little Engine That Could, by Watty Piper

The Maggie B., by Irene Haas

Play with Me, by Maria Hall

For other suggestions, ask the children's librarian at your local public library, or the proprietor of a good children's book shop. Happy reading.

Making Books

Homemade books are special because they can be tailored to your toddler's specific interest. They're easy to make, too, since a book is nothing more than picture-covered pages bound along one margin. Make lots.

The following suggested books are made with paper pages, so they're best for shared reading, and for the toddler who can either turn pages himself or is content to let you do it. You might want to use homemade books with your baby, too. After all, they're cheap. But always supervise, because a baby might rip up pages and chew—or choke—on the paper.

You can buy the basic supplies—report covers and punched paper—at any office supply or stationery store.

○

GREAT BOOKS!

Ideal Intro Age: 12 Months
Age Range: 12 to 36 Months

Tools & Materials

For each book:

- Heavy paper report cover, with fasteners that accept 3-hole-punched paper
- Several sheets of 3-hole-punched paper
- Magazines and other sources of pictures
- Scissors
- Cellophane (Scotch) tape

Directions

Fill the report cover with paper to make a blank book, then fill the pages with pictures you tape on. Suggested themes:

- Holiday Book: Cover the pages with old greeting cards. These usually have bright colors, glitter, embossed fronts, cutouts, and other sight-and-touch things toddlers love. Plus, each is a "mini-book" your toddler can open and close before going on to the next.

- Vacation Book: Fill with postcards you've picked up on vacation, and with snapshots you've taken. If your toddler accompanied you, this book will be a nice reminder that lets him relive the experience. If he didn't, this is a consolation that helps him feel involved, at least vicariously.

- Supermarket Book: A book of labels from packages of favorite foods. Cut them from magazine advertisements or from the package itself. When you and your toddler go shopping, let him find the real packages on the shelves.

- All About Me: A book with pictures of your toddler's favorite things; and, of course, of your toddler himself! Let him help choose the pictures to be included.

MORE LANGUAGE PLAY

○ Not all stories are in books. Make up your own, some with your toddler as the thinly disguised hero. You can plagiarize plots from familiar fairy tales.

○ Not all pictures are in books. Give your toddler a small box filled with pictures—old photographs, postcards, giveaways and other advertising material that comes through the mail. He'll love dumping them out, sorting through them, and putting them away. Play with him when you can, and talk about each pictured object.

○ Toddlers love lifting flaps in books to see what's behind them. Toddlers also love guessing the name when you point to an object and ask, "What's that?" Combine these two interests into one Surprise Picture Board. You slip a sheet of pictures inside the folder; your toddler opens the flaps one by one as you ask him, "What's that?"

○

SURPRISE PICTURE BOARD

Ideal Intro Age: 18 Months
Age Range: 18 to 36 Months

Tools & Materials

○ Letter-sized file folder

○ Several sheets of blank paper

○ Magazines and other sources of pictures

○ Ruler

○ Mat or hobby knife

○ Scissors

○ Cellophane (Scotch) tape

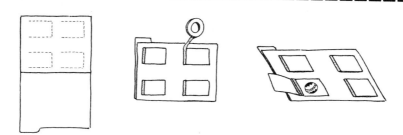

Directions

1. Open the file folder flat. Use the ruler and mat knife to cut four windows on the cover, as illustrated. Cut only three sides; the uncut side becomes the hinge.
2. Bend back each flap to make the hinge. Reinforce the hinges with tape, on both the facing and the reverse side.
3. On each sheet of paper, tape four pictures in places that correspond with the windows. These can be photographs, postcards, pictures cut from magazines and catalogues or off toy boxes, things you draw, whatever.
4. To play, shut the file folder and slide a picture sheet inside. Your toddler opens a flap—and guesses the object or person.

TO SUM UP

Language has been called the most powerful, most versatile resource of civilization. Little wonder that a baby is born with a predisposition for learning it. And little wonder that parents value its development so highly. By creating a rich verbal environment for your child, through the ways suggested here and countless others of your invention, you're helping him learn one of his most valuable tools.

WATER & SAND PLAY

"No, no, keep your fingers out of the pudding!"

"Mustn't play with that—it's dirty!"

Sound familiar? Probably, because most young children relish messy play, partly because they truly *are* messy—they lack skilled coordination and self-restraint—and partly because it's so much fun just to explore squishy, sloppy, ever-changing materials.

One beauty of water and sand (and mud and dirt) play is that these materials are so unstructured. There's no right way to use them, nor any wrong way except maybe throwing or eating them. With them your child can explore freely. The resulting mess is not only unpunished, it's expected. And because the play is so free-form, water and sand are a nice counterbalance to the more structured toys your young child also enjoys. There are plenty more benefits, too, and lots of ways to expand water and sand play.

PLAYING WITH WATER

A baby plays with water almost from the first time she takes a bath. She waves her arm—something moves and plops lightly against her skin. Later she kicks—more movement, more sensations. These early explorations give way to the scooping, pouring, and scientific experimentation that mark true water play.

Most babies enjoy true water play once they can sit securely in the tub, usually around 7 or 8 months if you use a plastic baby bath. The family tub is usually too slippery unless there is a rubber mat on the bottom. Once a baby is over this hurdle, water play becomes a joyful activity.

It has enormous benefit as well. While playing with water, your young child:

- Practices all kinds of arm-hand-finger skills and eye-hand coordination—splashing, filling, scooping, pouring, catching a bobbing object or a pouring stream.

- Learns scores of new words when you participate—*empty, full, wet, dry, float, sink, cold, warm.*

- Discovers early scientific principles, such as flotation and water power. ("What happens when I pour water over this paddle wheel?")

Water inspires fantasy play. For example, your toddler will probably bathe a baby doll (just as she herself is bathed) or wash up the play dishes after a tea party. Your suggestions and encouragement expand the possibilities. For example, invite your toddler to pretend she's a mermaid, a fish, a tugboat, the Loch Ness Monster, or any sea creature from one of her favorite books.

Teachers and play specialists note that water play can be very relaxing. Teachers often engage the excited or overeager child in a session at the water table. The feeling of the medium and the calming flow of water help relieve anxiety. Joy Goldberger, a specialist in play with the handicapped and hospitalized child, points out that water play is particularly effective for calming children who are unhappy at being hospitalized, or for relaxing children with muscular tension.

One other point. Water play makes a child feel successful. It requires no prescribed set of skills so there's no built-in potential of failure. It allows the child to experiment at her own pace, to succeed without pressure. The successes make the child feel confident; through confidence she's encouraged to try other things. Some become the skills that let her feel increasingly independent and self-confident. For example, through scooping and pouring water in play, a child practices the skills that let her pour her own cup of juice from the pitcher when she's a preschooler. So water play is, indeed, much more than just a bit of splashing and fun. But fun it is, too!

How can you help? Set up play opportunities, supervise to make sure everything's going safely, provide interesting props, offer verbal encouragement and new words—like *warm* and *cold, float* and *sink,* and so on—for her to learn, and (of course) join in when you can.

SAFETY NOTES

1. *Never* let your child play in or around water without your vigilant supervision. There's always a chance of drowning.
2. *Always* drain a wading pool or other container after playtime. Any body of standing water is a drowning hazard—to other neighborhood children as well as your own child.

3. *Never* let your child play in the bathroom unless you're there. She could drown in the toilet bowl.

Outdoor Play

○ A traditional wading pool is a favorite for outdoor water play. The molded plastic type is much more durable than the inflatable-ring type. (See the special homemade Sand & Sea Playground, page 152.)

○ For more confined spaces, or times you don't want to use the wading pool, fill a large tub with water. Your child sits outside it to play—or even inside if the tub accommodates both her and some favorite water toys. A large plastic washtub or the old plastic baby bath is a good container.

○ For even more confined play, fill a plastic dishpan. This is good for water play on a small porch, or for days when it's not warm enough for your child to sit in the water herself.

○ Let your toddler play with a hose, or frisk around under a sprinkler. *Special idea:* Train a sprinkler so it drizzles your toddler when she's in her wading pool. Fantasy rain!

Indoor Play

○ The bathtub is a natural. Store favorite bath toys in a drawstring mesh bag, and hang it on the shower head between playtimes so the toys drip dry. Or store toys in a plastic bucket on the bathroom floor, and drain it frequently.

○ Tub play needn't be limited to bathtime. Let your toddler play in the water-filled tub anytime that you need to be in the bathroom for a bit; for example, when you give it a thorough cleaning or fix a leaky faucet or set your hair.

○ Another idea. Your toddler can sit in a dry tub or the shower stall and play with water that's in a bucket or dishpan. She stays fairly dry, and so does the bathroom.

○ For more bathroom play: When you want to take a bath and your toddler is at the stage where she can't let you out of her sight (or you can't let *her* out of *your* sight), set her up with a dishpan of water and some toys on the bathroom floor. Her splashes will be easy to clean up.

○ If you can trust your older toddler to be careful, let her play with a container of water on a low table in the kitchen. Extra fun: Add a squirt of dishwashing liquid to the water, and give your toddler a wire whisk so she can beat the water into a sudsy froth.

The baby bath, set into the family tub, can help the newly sitting baby feel more confident for water play.

Set up some water play on the bathroom floor when *you* want a nice long relaxing bath.

Good Water Toys

○ Plastic kitchen items like cups with handles, sieves and strainers, plastic sifter, and measuring cups.

○ Sponges.

○ Non-waterloggable balls.

○ Length of plastic tubing, if your toddler knows the difference between blowing and sipping.

○ *Clean* squirt bottles, small enough for your toddler to hold and squeeze.

○ Commercial water toys; those that manipulate water a variety of ways, and that have removable parts that can be stacked and fitted together, will get extra play.

○

INFLATABLE TUB BOAT

This toy is designed for general water play and for fantasy. The tub is a good container for filling with water via small cups. The holes make it a giant sieve; your toddler will love lifting up this toy to see the water sprinkle out. It can give rides to dolls and other seafaring passengers in make-believe scenarios, too.
Ideal Intro Age: 12 Months
Age Range: 12 to 36 Months

Tools & Materials

○ Inflatable water ring ("life preserver")

○ Plastic tub (ice cream or margarine container) that fits snugly inside the ring

○ Hammer and large nail

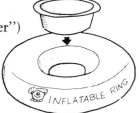

INFLATABLE RING

Directions

1. Use the hammer and large nail to punch several holes in the bottom of the plastic tub.
2. Inflate the water ring and wedge the tub into the open center.

PLAYING WITH SAND

Sand is a rather magic material. Because it can be scooped and poured like water, it offers many of water's benefits: skill development, concept learning, new vocabulary words. But it has special qualities. It can be dribbled into interesting patterns. It's good for drawing in, digging in, and hiding toys in. Add water and it becomes like dough that holds its shape when pressed and formed. Or you can press cookie cutters into it to make designs. Add more water and it becomes runny. Not really a solid, not really a liquid, it's somewhere else instead.

Sand is magical—not really solid, not really liquid.

One family turned a giant tractor tire into a sandbox. For another idea, see the homemade Sand & Sea Playground.

Good Sand Toys

Most water toys (cups, sieves, etc.); serving spoon or small shovel for digging; drumsticklike rod for drawing; plastic cookie cutters; and toy vehicles and characters for the older toddler.

SAFETY NOTES

1. Always supervise sandbox play. Your child might try to eat or throw the sand.
2. If you use a neighborhood sandbox, sift through it before your child plays. Neighborhood animals (especially cats) have a habit of using a sandbox for a toilet. Keep your home sandbox covered with a plastic sheet weighted in the corners, or a sheet of plywood.

The following homemade twin-pooled Sand & Sea Playground takes care of the cover question nicely. One pool is turned into a sandbox, the other is used as a wading pool/sandbox lid. Admittedly, this idea is *not* inexpensive. However, if you're planning to buy or build a sandbox anyway, this one is very easy. And the extra wading pool/lid gives it much more play opportunity. Remember, too, that a sandbox and wading pool remain favorite toys throughout the early years.

SAND & SEA PLAYGROUND

Ideal Intro Age: 9 Months
Age Range: 9 to 36 Months
FOR SUPERVISED PLAY ONLY

Tools & Materials

- 2 molded plastic wading pools, each with a rolled lip around the perimeter

- 3 wood planks, each about 4' long, about 4" wide, and at least 1" thick

- Builders sand—plenty

- Electric drill and large bit (at least ¼")

- 2 large, strong spring-type clamps or large "C" clamps

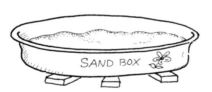

Directions

1. Decide where you want the sandbox to be located; once it's installed it will be hard to move. Some tips:

   - The ground should be level.

   - Ideally, the spot should be partially shaded. If your baby likes to play in the sand for long periods, the sandbox (and she) can get very hot when totally exposed to the sun.

2. Drill several water-drainage holes in the bottom of one pool (this will be the sandbox).

3. Set the sandbox on the three planks. These raise it slightly off the ground, so any water that gets inside can drain out.

4. Fill with sand, at least four inches deep.

5. Use the other pool as a conventional wading pool. It's best not to set it too near the sandbox, though, or your child will probably delight in pouring water from the pool into the sandbox.

6. When playtime's over, lay the wading pool upside down on top of the sandbox, and clamp the two rims together. This lid keeps cats and rainwater out of the sand.

SAFETY NOTE: The clamps are NOT suitable toys; keep them away from your child.

TO SUM UP

Water and sand, like the early art supplies discussed in Chapter 3, Activities for Hands (and Heads), are usually considered creative materials, since they give free rein to a child's imagination. The next chapter looks at another creative part of your young child's life—music.

SOUND & MUSIC

Babies and toddlers are as fascinated by things that they hear as things they see and touch. Many child development experts label children as naturally musical. Babies can hear right from birth (actually, even in the womb), and enjoy listening to sounds and music from the first weeks. It's obvious they like hearing parents sing; traditionally, babies have been soothed to sleep with lullabyes. Older babies coo and babble rhythmically without any encouragement. They bounce and sway to music and love to make sounds with toys. Toddlers march and dance spiritedly; join in songs that have a familiar, catchy verse; make their own abstract music with an assortment of simple instruments. As Donna Brink Fox, a children's music expert at the Eastman School of Music, recently pointed out,

In fact, there seems to be no way to prevent children from displaying these musical behaviors, for during the preschool years music becomes both a means and an end, a fun way to help learn things, but also a purely expressive behavior important for its own sake.

Like your baby's other abilities, there are several ways you can enjoy and enhance this inborn interest through play.

SETTING THE MUSICAL STAGE

Whether you want to sow the seeds of a musical career or merely to enlarge all your child's horizons, *your* interest in music likely affects his own.

Researchers Jeanette Jenkins, William Kirkpatrick, and others have found a consistent relationship between musical development and the home environment. Put simply, a child whose parents value music, who listen to music frequently and play musical parent-child games, generally has an increased enjoyment in and aptitude for music. This is similar to the situation regarding early readers—they tend to come from homes where parents read a lot both in general and with their child. In such cases, parents are role models. When you spend time involved in music, and particularly when you share music with your child, you tell him that such activities are valued.

This general influence also has theoretical connections with true music talent that may surface in later years. Music researcher Benjamin Bloom conducted a comprehensive study of talented young people, looking at many aspects of their backgrounds. His report concluded that "Extremely talented people aren't born with extraordinary gifts. More likely, they

Your own interest in music is probably your child's greatest motivation.

○ 155 ○

become highly talented because of the way their parents raise them and the atmosphere in their homes."

EARLY BEGINNINGS

Hearing is the obvious foundation of music appreciation and development, and this sense is working even before birth. From about the fourth or fifth month of pregnancy, the unborn baby moves about more actively when his mother speaks loudly or makes a loud sound. Mothers-to-be have reported increased movement, too, when they type at an electric typewriter or have their teeth drilled by the dentist.

Some experts believe that a baby is influenced by such early experiences in the womb, and even recalls them after he's born. There's anecdotal evidence that pieces of music may become imprinted *in utero.* As pediatrician T. Berry Brazelton related in a magazine article:

> A woman who is a pianist claims that she practiced a Chopin waltz over and over in the last month of her pregnancy. After the baby came she stopped playing, and it was not until he was 3 months old that she started again. One day she revived the Chopin waltz. Her baby had been kicking and gurgling in his playpen near the piano; when she began the waltz he stopped all activity, turned toward the piano and was transfixed. She is convinced that he remembered it. So am I.

In the delivery room a baby turns his head toward a sound and tries to discover where it is coming from. The newborn prefers human voices, and studies show that he can even distinguish his mother's voice from those of other people (more evidence of prenatal stimulation!).

Babies not only hear; they can also distinguish between different sounds from a very early age. You probably see your baby react to various sounds in different ways. Sudden loud sounds and high-pitched squeaks (like a whistling tea kettle) may make him stiffen and cry. Calm, gentle sounds like a lullabye usually relax him. Experiments reveal that a baby's sound discrimination skills are even sharper than these everyday observable reactions. From about 8 weeks, babies in a research setting could tell the difference between two tones fairly close in pitch. Six-month-olds could perceive changes in melodies. All this laboratory and popular evidence suggests that babies are never too young to enjoy, "interpret," and in some way respond to sound and music.

GENERAL PLAY TIPS

○ Let your baby listen to all the types of music you enjoy, from classical to rock, country to pop, jazz and Broadway and opera and everything in between. Sometimes music can be the focus of your experience—for instance, you and your baby might rock together in the rocking chair while listening to some relaxing piece. Or you might dance and sway together while listening to music with an upbeat tempo. Other times, music might serve more as accompaniment. As mentioned elsewhere in this book, rhythmic music can be used to enhance an exercise routine or some spirited jumping play.

While you're at it, take your baby on a cultural tour of music you yourself might never have really listened to. Try ethnic music from other lands, religious music, tribal and folk songs, medieval chants and avant-garde composition. Most public libraries have a range of musical records and tapes that you can borrow.

Pay attention to your baby's response to the music you play. Some children are agitated by loud music, or music with uneven or unusual rhythms. Then again, every child has personal tastes, and your baby won't necessarily like everything that you might.

○ Consider putting a radio in the nursery. Quiet instrumental music might calm your fussy baby and help him fall asleep on fretful nights.

○ Your older baby might enjoy sitting on the floor and swaying to music, especially when you do it, too. Or hold him in the standing position so that he can bounce and "dance" along to the rhythm. Or pick him up and dance together. Waltz. Jounce. Zip and twirl.   ○ 157 ○

Or when he can stand alone, hold his hands and dance like partners.

○ Your toddler loves to dance alone as well as with you. Just turn on the radio or stereo and let him devise his own choreography.

○ Remember those musical resources outside the home, like seasonal parades. Most young children love marching music (as long as they are far enough away so that the music isn't too loud). Does your local high school have a marching band? Find out when they rehearse outdoors, and ask if you can attend. You and your child might have a nice picnic while listening.

○ And don't forget that your singing adds terrifically personal music to your baby's world. You'll probably never have a more enraptured, appreciative audience.

○ Make a few songs part of the bedtime routine.

○ When your young child is getting fidgety in his carseat, launch into some favorite familiar tune, especially one that has lots of repetition ("Old MacDonald," "Yankee Doodle," "She'll Be Comin' Round the Mountain When She Comes"). If you encourage him, he might join in, too—croon, babble, or sing a few words, depending on his skill level.

Help your young baby dance—maybe in tandem with a favorite cloth toy.

○ Teachers I know often bring chants and invented songs into many other activities. For example, they chant "This is the way we wash our hands" (to the tune of "Here We Go Round the Mulberry Bush") when cleaning toddlers' hands after arts play. Or they sing stories, or parts of stories, instead of speaking them. These can be very simple words and tunes—or even familiar tunes with new words inserted. Teachers find that singing helps hold the baby's attention and enhances his developing vocabulary. Simple tunes can make it easier to learn and remember words. Chances are that you memorized the alphabet to the tune of "Twinkle Twinkle, Little Star." It's no secret that adults, too, often recall advertising lyrics more easily and powerfully than merely spoken statements.

NURSERY RHYMES

Nursery rhymes combine singing (or chanting), movement, close contact with beloved parents, and elements of surprise. No wonder they've been cherished for centuries.

There are thousands of rhymes, enough to fill a book. Or really, several books, because there are many nursery rhyme books available. I recommend you buy one. Until you have a chance, though, here are some favorite rhymes to get you started.

○ Make a fist. Chant this counting rhyme, exposing one finger at a time.

> Here is a beehive—where are the bees?
> Hidden away where nobody sees.
> Soon they come creeping out of the hive—
> One! Two! Three! Four! Five!

○ Pull your baby's fingers or toes in turn as you recite "This Little Piggie."

○ With your baby lying on his back, or sitting in your lap facing you, pull his arms back and forth in a chug-a-chug motion while reciting "Row, Row, Row Your Boat."

○ Help your baby clap his hands as you sing "Pat-a-cake, Pat-a-cake, Baker's Man." Insert your baby's name in the last line: "And put it in the oven for *Stephen* and me." Poke him gently in the stomach when you reach his name. Soon he'll begin anticipating this tickly finale with mounting excitement.

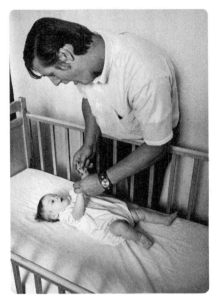

Pull your baby's arms in a chug-a-chug fashion to the words of "Row, Row, Row Your Boat."

○ "Rock-a-bye Baby" is definitely among the top ten rhymes, if not the Hit Parade No. 1. Here's one way to enjoy it. Sit your baby in your lap, facing you, and hold him around the waist. While you sing the first three lines, rock him from side to side. When the bough breaks, of course, the cradle will fall. On the word *fall,* suddenly help your baby fall backwards slightly, then bring him back to sitting position. Once he has the hang of this version, let him fall further and further back. The variation adds to the surprise. You can also hold his hands rather than waist—but hang on tight when he falls!

○ Sit with your baby on the floor and chant "Pop Goes the Weasel." Again, sway him from side to side until—*pop;* then lift him slightly off the floor.

○ Bounce your baby on your knees (keeping toes on the floor, raise and lower your heels) while you chant a riding rhyme, such as:

Ride a cock horse to Banbury Cross,
To see a fair lady upon a white horse.
With rings on her fingers and bells on her toes,
She shall have music wherever she goes.

○ Your older baby and toddler also likes watching you perform little finger plays in synchrony with an appropriate ditty. Favorites are "Itsy Bitsy Spider" (or "Eensy Weensy Spider") and "Where Is Thumbkin?" A good simple finger-play songbook is worthwhile, too. Note: Each slim volume in the *Wee Sing* series comes with a cassette tape of the songs in the book.

FIRST INSTRUMENTS

Your baby's first musical instruments are all those soundmakers—rattles, bell-type toys, any kind of shakers—described in Chapter 3, Activities for Hands (and Heads). Even before he is old enough to play with these himself, he likes hearing you make sounds with them.

From about 6 or 7 months, your baby beats on a drumlike object with his hands or an appropriate drumstick.

○ Good drums: cooking pots or plastic mixing bowls turned upside down, small cardboard boxes, series of upside down aluminum baking pans.

○ Good drumsticks: Cooking spoons (metal or wooden), small wooden mallet, hand-held rattles (they make a rattle sound and a clumping sound!). It's best to supervise play with any drumstick that has a small end your baby might put into his mouth.

Your toddler is ready for simple rhythm band instruments—maracas, cymbals, rhythm sticks, a xylophone, and the like. Have a parade—you, your toddler, and any other children and adults available can march around clanging and shaking and tooting and ringing. It may not sound like music to you, but from cacophony comes modern symphonies.

BAND INSTRUMENTS

Ideal Intro Age: 15 Months
Age Range: 15 to 36 Months

Tools & Materials

○ Various things, depending on the instruments you make

Directions:

1. Clappers: Screw D-shaped cabinet handles onto two blocks of wood, each about 6″ long, 3″ wide, and 1″ thick.
2. Rhythm Sticks: Cut two pieces of wooden doweling, each about 12″ long and 1″ in diameter; your toddler beats these together.
3. Shakers: Fill a metal screw-top spice shaker with some jar lids too large for your toddler to put into his mouth (in case he should open the shaker). Other favorite: *loud* baby rattle.
4. Cymbals: Screw a wooden cabinet knob on the bottom outside of each of a pair of aluminum pie plates. Other favorite: Two cooking pot lids that don't have rims on the underside.
5. Drum: Give your toddler a small cooking pot and a wooden mallet beater.

HINT: Cooking pots and lids and baking pans are wonderful instruments, but constant music play will dent and batter them. It makes sense to buy your toddler his own set at the thrift shop or flea market. If you like, store these and other instruments in a large cardboard box with appropriate decorations—musical notes, a drum, etc.—on the outside. Draw them with markers, or cut pictures from magazines and glue on.

SAFETY NOTE: Sand down the rough edges of all pieces of wood. Surfaces should be smooth to the touch and all corners should be rounded.

CHILDREN'S RECORDS

Besides all the recorded music *you* like, your toddler enjoys some special children's records with simple songs and musical activities geared for his age group. These are also fun for you and him to listen to together; and they'll give you ideas of other musical games appropriate for toddlers. The best source I know is the marvelous mail-order company and store called Children's Book and Music Center. Write for a free catalogue. And should you have any questions about a record, the staff is excellently trained and wonderfully helpful. As of this writing, the address is:

> Children's Book and Music Center
> 2500 Santa Monica Boulevard
> Santa Monica, CA 90404

TO SUM UP

Early music is many things: from your baby's first cry to rhythmic cooing and babbling to singing snatches of songs along with you; from tentatively shaking a rattle to marching about beating a drum; from listening to a soothing lullabye to clapping his hands along with a "Songs for Toddlers" record. Music has charms that soothe the savage breast or infectiousness that inspires inventive movement. It's personal and it's social, a part of each culture's heritage. And through such early music play as described here, you're helping to pass it along.

THAT'S ME!

The early years are a time of learning, and one topic that particularly interests your toddler is *herself.* Who am I? What do I look like? What am I comprised of? What makes me unique? This process of self-discovery, or self-recognition as it's sometimes called, begins when she's born and never really ends. We grow and change and discover ourselves throughout life.

As parents you are responsible for helping your child develop a strong and positive image of herself. One way you do this is by providing a solid sense of security, so that she views the world as a safe and secure place. This you give through care, support, nurturing, encouragement, praise, sympathy, understanding—in sum, through love and all it entails. These things a book can't teach.

Another, more prosaic way is by helping her learn about herself—what she looks like, the names and functions of parts of her body, an idea of her own unique being.

Your child is your companion on her self-discovery adventure. Everything she does helps her learn about herself—what she can and cannot do, what she likes and dislikes. Throughout these early years she also exhibits behaviors—some endearing, some baffling, some even seemingly negative—that enhance and reflect her developing sense of self. Here are some highlights, and ways you can help her learn *"That's me!"*

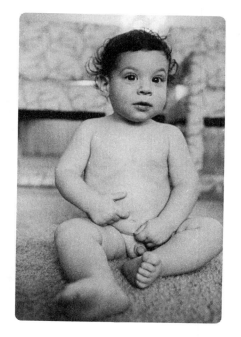

WHAT AM I MADE OF?

Starting at about 1 or 2 months, your baby occasionally glances at her own outstretched hand as it passes through her line of vision. Most developmental psychologists believe that at this early age, she doesn't realize it's a part of her any more or less than she thinks a toy is a part of her. But within a few months she stares at her hand more deliberately, and plays with her own hands and fingers. By now she has also experienced holding and releasing objects. It's believed that she can now distinguish between what is her and what isn't.

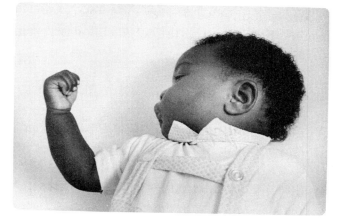

A young baby isn't really sure whether her hand is part of her.

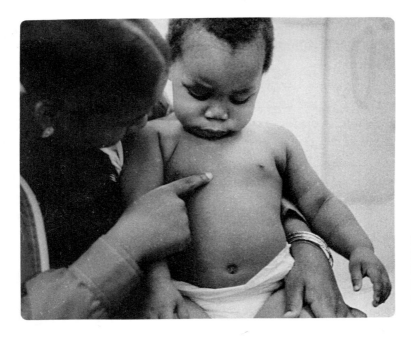

Naming games help your baby learn who she is and what she's made of.

Starting around 5 or 6 months, a baby explores not only her hands, but also her feet, hair, nose, ears, genitals—every part of her body within reach. This continues well into the toddler years as she seeks to learn what each part feels like and how it works.

The best way to help her learn about her body is the simple naming game that almost every parent instinctively plays. As you point to and name each part of her face and body, add a few words about its function. "This is your nose, Jessica. We smell things with our nose." Naming games are ideal for bathtime, changing time, almost anytime you two play together.

WHAT'S MY NAME?

Your baby's name is a distinctive part of her individuality. Use it often when you speak to her. Near the end of her first year she links her name to herself, and points to herself correctly when asked "Where's (baby's name)?" Most children begin calling themselves by their name at around 2 years of age.

WHO'S IN THAT MIRROR?

A mirror helps your baby learn what she looks like, so make mirror games part of playtimes together.

○ Put a large, unbreakable mirror in your baby's crib. She's fascinated by her reflection because this "picture" is always different. And it moves. Attach the mirror securely to cribside so it doesn't topple over.

○ Let your 2- or 3-month-old look into a hand mirror. Talk about the different parts of her face. Starting at about 6 months or so, she might like to pat, talk to, and even kiss her new friend.

○ Hold your baby up so she can see herself in wall mirrors, too. Or help her sit on a dresser so she can see herself in the bureau mirror. Don't leave her alone, though.

○ Play some mirror peekaboo. Hold your baby in your lap and position a hand mirror where she can see her face. Tilt it so she disappears: "Where's Carla?" Tilt it back so she reappears with "There's Carla. There she is! Peekaboo!"

○ From about 9 months on, hold your baby in your arms as you dance together in front of a full length mirror. She enjoys watching as well as feeling the action.

○ Don't forget—that three-way dressing mirror in a department store is particularly fascinating. It creates three babies at once.

Does She Know Who It Is?

At what age does a baby looking in a mirror realize that she's seeing herself rather than "another baby?" The answer isn't absolute, but here's some evidence.

One study by researcher Tiffany Brown placed 3-month-olds face to face with a mirror and with another baby the same age. On the whole,   ○ 167 ○

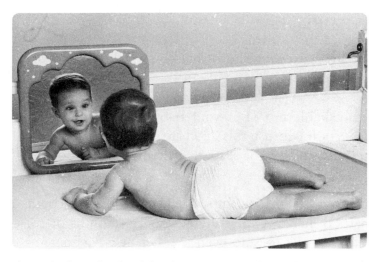

At what age does a baby recognize herself? Probably between 18 and 24 months.

these babies looked for longer periods at the mirror but interacted more with the live infants. This suggests that a 3-month-old can tell the difference between a reflected image and a real baby, but it doesn't prove that the subjects knew they were looking at themselves.

In a study by psychologists Bennett Berthenthal and Kurt Fischer, each parent dressed her baby in a special vest that supported a hat about six inches above the baby's head. (At this point, the baby did not realize the hat existed.) Then the baby was placed in front of a mirror, and the parent drew attention to the reflected hat and asked her baby to find it. The researchers reasoned that if a baby looked or reached up at the real hat, rather than trying to grab the reflected image, she must have known it was she—not another baby—in that mirror.

The babies in this study searched correctly at about 10 months on average. But again, did this mean the babies recognized themselves, or did they just know the difference between a real baby and a reflected one?

A simple and clever study was devised. Each mother-baby pair was brought into the laboratory where the mother secretly dabbed a spot of rouge on her baby's nose. Then the baby was placed in front of a mirror. If the baby pointed to or touched or otherwise examined the spot, the researchers reasoned, then she must realize she's looking at herself. Here's what the researchers found:

- Babies from 6 to about 14 months cooed and babbled and patted their reflections, but none examined the spot.

- About half of the 18- to 20-month-olds examined the spot, demonstrating that they recognized themselves.

- Nearly two-thirds of the 21- to 24-month-olds recognized themselves.

In another examination by Berthenthal and Fischer, each child looked into a mirror while her mother pointed to the reflection and asked "Who's that?" If the child stated her name or used an appropriate pronoun she was judged as recognizing herself. On the average, this happened at 24 months.

So when does your child recognize herself in the mirror? Probably between 18 and 24 months. Another study found that children recognize themselves in photographs at about the same age, too.

"SECURITY BLANKETS"

Another way a child exhibits her growing sense of self is by adopting a security blanket.

As discussed in Peekaboo, page 50, after 6 months a baby begins to realize that she is separate and distinct from her parents, and as she grows increasingly independent, she suffers bouts of insecurity. During these temporary travails she often turns for comfort to a pacifier, her thumb, or a favorite "security blanket" when you aren't available.

Cuddlies and loveys—a blanket, a stuffed animal, an old soft cloth—are quite common. A recent survey found that about 60 percent of the 18-month-olds studied had a favorite cuddly. An almost identical proportion of 3-year-olds in the same study were still attached to cuddlies.

A cuddly is so popular because it serves, in the words of child development specialist D. W. Winnicott, as a "transitional object." This nice, familiar friend helps a child weather the transition from complete emotional dependence on her parents to partial independence. By relying on a cuddly, your child shows that she is developing her own mechanisms for dealing with stress and insecurity. The pediatrician T. Berry Brazelton lauds them, too:

> I am always gratified when children form attachments to objects. . . . It gives them one more advantage in coping with the rigors of growing up, with all its frustrations and necessary separations from mother.

In fact, another study found that a cuddly is just as effective as the mother's presence in helping a toddler adjust to unfamiliar situations. So if your child adopts one, be sure to carry it with you whenever she might face some situation that might trouble her, especially if you can't be with her every moment.

Keep in mind that not all children adopt a cuddly. As mentioned above, some rely on their thumb, a pacifier, or activities like rhythmic rocking or fingering and twisting their hair to help get through temporary rough times.

The Huggable Butterfly, one of the simplest homemade stuffed toys I know, is a good candidate for becoming a favorite security blanket. It's bright and colorful, easy to grasp and hug, and the terry texture is quite comforting.

HUGGABLE BUTTERFLY

Ideal Intro Age: 6 Months
Age Range: 6 to 36 Months

Tools & Materials

- 2 hand towels, each no larger than 12″ × 18″; choose ones with broad stripes or other bold patterns

- Piece of thick, soft yarn, at least 24″ long

- Polyester fiberfill, shredded foam, or other machine-washable stuffing
- Sewing machine or needle and thread

Directions

1. Place the towels together, with the patterned sides (if any) face to face, and sew around 3 sides.
2. Turn this pocket right-side-out again, stuff tightly, and sew closed the remaining side to create a pillow.
3. Loop the yarn two or three times around the center of this pillow, pull *tight* to form two butterfly "wings," and knot *securely* with a double or triple knot.
4. Trim off the excess yarn, right down to the knot.

IS IT SELFISHNESS?

"Me!" "Mine!" At some point these become your toddler's watchcries. Are they, as many parents fear, the sign of escalating selfishness? Usually not. They're merely another way your toddler reveals her developing sense of self.

At some point during her second year, your toddler starts recognizing that some objects are *hers,* while others are *Daddy's* or *Mummy's* or *Sister's,* and emphatically distinguishes between "mine!" and "yours." Sometimes this sense of possession will prompt shouts of *"No!"* when another person, especially a sibling or peer, tries to play with her toys.

Rather than piggishness, these outbursts reflect a toddler's insecure sense of personal identity. Since one way she defines herself is through her possessions—*my* shoes, *my* coat, *my* toys—she naturally feels a bit threatened when a part of herself is snatched away. Over time, though, she'll develop a fuller, more mature understanding of herself, and will be more relaxed about sharing her worldly goods. This will be a sign that she's becoming more secure in her newfound identity.

But why does she have to be so possessive at first, you might ask. Well, think about other skills she's been developing—skills like walking or saying a first word. At every new milestone she tended to overdo it a bit. The same is true about the steps in discovering herself.

ALL ABOUT ME

Here are some additional ways to help your toddler learn all about herself.

Family Photo Albums

Share with your toddler family albums filled with pictures that chronicle her life: the pregnant mother, coming home from the hospital or birthing center, first birthday, and all the other moments you've captured on film. Remind her that once she was a little baby, "But you're such a big girl now!" Talk about other family members, too, using appropriate titles like Grandmother and Aunt and Brother, so she understands a bit about her family as well.

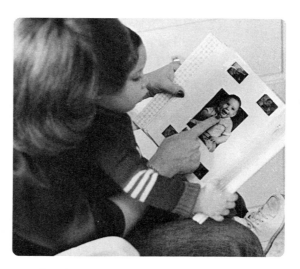

Family photo albums help your child learn about herself and her connection to other family members.

○　**WALL-LINE SCRAPBOOK**

This novel room decoration spells out highlights of your toddler's past in an easy-to-follow sequential format. Hold her in your arms and go down the line, talking about each picture or object displayed. Naturally, she won't understand the signifi-

cance of this presentation for months, but it's a nice way to tell a living story. And over time she will learn what it means.
Ideal Intro Age: 12 Months
Age Range: 12 to 36 Months

Tools & Materials

- Photographs and various favorite items
- Several pinch-type clothespins
- Long piece of clothesline
- 2 hooks

Directions

1. Thread clothespins onto the clothesline.
2. Tie a loop in each end of the clothesline, and hang it up on hooks screwed into the wall. The line itself should be about level with your head.
3. From the clothespins, hang photographs that represent, in order, some important events in your child's life. Among the photographs intersperse favorite baby toys and articles of clothing—a T-shirt, first socks and shoes—that help your toddler understand how big she's growing. Add new items as new milestones pass, too.

MY BODY POSTER

This nursery wall decoration can help your toddler learn the printed names for different body parts. And since it's a poster of her, it has built-in appeal.
Ideal Intro Age: 24 Months
Age Range: 24 to 36 Months

Tools & Materials

- Piece of paper at least 3' wide and slightly longer than your child is tall (you may need to tape together several sheets to make one this size)

- Pencil

- Crayons or felt-tipped markers

- Masking tape

Directions

1. Lay the paper flat on a hard floor.
2. Help your toddler lie on her back on the paper. It's best if she's nude or in underwear. Trace around her body with the pencil.
3. Help her stand up, then retrace the outline with a crayon or marker.
4. Add finishing details: Print the names of body parts in large block letters; color in some hair; add facial features, nipples, and belly-button; delineate toes.
5. Hang on the wall with tape, low enough so that the drawn feet touch the floor. This way your child can match herself to her poster.

HINT: Do posters of all the children—Mom and Dad, too. Hang them side by side so you can compare heights.

TO SUM UP

Now that you've helped your child learn who she is, let's look at things she might be. It's time for some fantasy.

THE BEGINNINGS OF FANTASY

Older toddlers and preschoolers slip quite easily and naturally into make-believe. They're Mommies and Daddies who care for a brood of assorted dolls, stuffed animals, and other nice and naughty children. They're doctors and nurses, grocery store clerks and mail carriers, police officers and firefighters, even (as they get older) the superheroes they see on television. In short, they play the roles of any familiar adult who (in their eyes) is wise, powerful, and respected. There are ways that you can help this budding fantasy flourish with the props and play suggestions in this chapter.

HOW FANTASY DEVELOPS

The roots of fantasy play lie in the simple imitation games of infancy. At different ages, a baby imitates his parents' facial expressions (for instance, sticking out his tongue), gestures such as waving bye-bye, and actions like giving a kiss or playing pat-a-cake. Sometimes the parent initiates the exchange, other times the baby does. But whatever the imitation, it happens only while both parent and baby are present and actively involved.

A toddler imitates more complicated adult activities. He dusts and sweeps as he has seen his parents do. He pretends to drive a car, or picks up a briefcase and parades around like he's Daddy. He also acts out little routines with which he's familiar: "drinking" from an empty cup, "eating" with an empty spoon, "washing" his face with a dry cloth. The difference between these activities and the earlier ones is more than their complexity. He performs them even when a parent is *not* playing with him. Rather than needing a direct role model, he mimics from memory.

Between 18 and 24 months, he adds a dramatic shift to simple imitation play. Now he performs familiar routines on dolls and stuffed animals as well as himself. He washes and feeds his doll, puts it to bed and hugs it when it "cries"; that is, he does to the doll what parents usually do to him. He might take toy characters for rides in a toy car or bus as he is often taken. In short, he assumes the role of a different person—usually an adult—and acts out what that familiar character does. This is the real beginning of the complex and fascinating fantasy play that's the hallmark of the preschool years. Soon it grows to include complicated plots, all kinds of abstract as well as real props, and other children.

Caring for his doll the same ways he is cared for by you marks a big shift in your toddler's fantasy development.

WHY SO IMPORTANT?

Experts (and parents) used to think that fantasy was at best a waste of time, at worst the sign of a troubled child, maybe even a child possessed. Today we take a lighter view. Fantasy is something that nearly every child does. And most experts agree that it has very positive attributes.

As your child grows, he ventures increasingly beyond the protection of his home and family. In his burgeoning independence he occasionally encounters things that confuse or trouble him—the bullying child next door, the doctor who (although as nice as can be) gives him a painful injection. Even developments at home can be disquieting, especially the arrival of a new baby. Parents, too, come and go according to their schedules, not his whims. It's not surprising that he suffers occasional insecurities.

One way a child deals with these insecurities is through fantasy. He becomes the brave fireman racing to extinguish the flames; he's the daredevil pilot swooping through the skies. On a more familiar note, he's the mailman or school bus driver or delivery man, the helpful and respected adult he sees in his own neighborhood. Or he's the Mommy or Daddy driving a child (himself!) to the store or day care center. These feelings of power and control, fleeting though they may be, help him feel strong and good about himself.

Naturally, you, his parents, are the most powerful people in your toddler's life, and the ones who exert the most control. When your toddler becomes the parent to a doll or stuffed animal, he enjoys this power, too.

A child works through some bad feelings in fantasy play. He recreates an unpleasant experience, but changes it to suit his whims. If he's angry in real life at the needle-wielding pediatrician, in his play he gives the doctor a shot. This makes him feel better. Or he takes out his momentary jealous feelings about his new baby sister on his uncomplaining teddy bear. This alleviates the need to act them out on his real sibling.

These fantasies of power are just that—fantasies. But the good feelings they bring are real, and they make your child feel more confident.

Fantasy has correlations with other skills, too. Studies show that chil-   o 177 o dren who engage in lots of fantasy play usually perform better than other children on thinking skills tests. They also tend to be better at entertaining themselves, usually have long attention spans, and have superior vocabulary skills.

Fantasy is also linked to that elusive term we call creativity. On the whole, children with active imaginations are more spontaneous, flexible, and able to adapt to new situations than less imaginative children. They also tend to offer more numerous and imaginative ideas in discussions. No one can assert whether fantasy leads to this creativity, or whether highly creative children just happen to like fantasy play, but the two are definitely linked.

FOSTERING FANTASY

Although you can't teach a child to be imaginative, you can encourage his natural talent for fantasy, say Dorothy and Jerome Singer. These specialists in play and especially make-believe, believe that, "While the capacity for fantasy or pretending is inherent in all reasonably normal human beings, the degree to which it is used by children depends to a large degree on whether parents or other adults have fostered it." You can foster it by:

- Enlarging your child's frame of reference;

- encouraging your child's imaginative thinking through play suggestions;

- taking part in his fantasy scenarios; and

- providing toys and props that lend themselves to make-believe play.

Enlarging Your Child's World

- Read to your toddler. Favorite books will surely become plots he'll later act out. Stories also carry him into fantasy worlds populated by talking cars and engines that can make it over the highest hill with a menagerie on board (*The Little Engine That Could*) and teddy bears who live like children (especially *Corduroy*).

○ Make up stories. Simple tales involving his doll or favorite stuffed animal. Stories about the magic bus in front of you as you drive to the market. Fables about the family pet. Tailor the length and complexity of these tales to your toddler's age and level of comprehension.

○ Go on outings. Trips to the zoo, the park, the library, the children's museum, the pet store, all inspire fantasy reenactment at home.

Encouraging Imaginative Thinking

○ Be imaginative yourself. Look at things differently. Help your toddler pretend even mundane things are magical. The vacuum cleaner is a dirt-eating dragon, the playground slide an ice-covered mountain, the car a rocket ship ("Everyone into his safety seat for blast-off!"). In the deparment store, the elevator is a time machine, the escalator magic stairs. "What will we find at the top?"

○ Make believe that you are different things. For instance, pretend you're a puppy. Ask your toddler to pet you just as he pets the family pooch. Can he be a dog, too? Can he woof like a dog? Or pretend you're the baby and *he's* the Daddy.

○ Offer words of encouragement and additional suggestions when your toddler is involved in a fantasy routine. Elaborate on what he's doing, and suggest new directions. If he's playing with dolly, offer something like "How nice, you're giving dolly a bath. Did you wash her hair? You'd better wash her hair. . . . Oh, dolly looks so tired now. I think she wants to go to bed. Can you put dolly to bed?" If he's pushing a truck around the floor, ask him: What kind of truck is it? What is it carrying? Is it an ice cream van? Can he sell you some ice cream? Where is it going now? Can

One way to encourage imaginative play—suggest and participate in fantasy scenarios.

he make it go to the store and pick up some more ice cream? Suggest that now it's a fire truck. Or a circus wagon. Is your toddler stirring some fantasy concoction in a pot? Suggest he make some soup, some vegetable soup made with blocks, some teddy bear soup, a tennis ball stew. Can he give you a taste?

FANTASY TOYS AND PROPS

Here are some suggested basic and not-so-basic fantasy toys. This list is by no means exhaustive; your toddler turns almost anything into a fantasy prop if it fits in with his scheme or plot.

Dolls and Stuffed Animals

Dolls and stuffed animals are the staples. The mainstay might be a nice, plain plastic baby doll with molded-on or rooted hair, because it stands up to being washed repeatedly, dunked in a mud puddle, thrown down the stairs, chewed on, covered with food, slammed against the door in a fit of anger. Stuffed animals also get pretty rough treatment at a toddler's hands, so they should be machine washable as well. A simple doll bed (a doll-sized cradle, a shoebox with a folded towel inside) and other plain, sturdy accessories extend fantasy scenarios. And when you join in and play family ("You're the Daddy and I'm the Mommy and dolly is our baby") the play possibilities are endless.

Dolls and stuffed animals (and appropriate accessories) are the heart of a younger toddler's make-believe.

Plastic Cups, Saucers, Plates

For tea parties with you, siblings, dolls and stuffed pets, or solitary meals your toddler wants to prepare. NOTE: The elaborate kitchen-type props—stove, refrigerator, etc.—are usually more appreciated by pre-schoolers than toddlers.

Role-playing Props

Since you are your child's absolute number one heroes, he'll most often pretend he's Mommy or Daddy. Provide props that he identifies with you: an old pocketbook or briefcase, a hat, a pair of sunglasses, gloves, slippers. Clothing and personal props like these should be easy for him to put on and off; when he's a preschooler, he'll be more interested in really dressing up in cast-off clothing.

BLUE JEANS BAG

This splendid toddler tote bag sparks lots of fantasy and toddler role playing; it becomes, among other things, a pocketbook or briefcase that makes a young child feel very grown up indeed. With its roomy center compartment and several pockets for stuffing things into, it's perfect for holding personal treasures. The button (or snap) and zipper let your toddler practice dressing skills. It fits right into games you and your toddler can play, too.

Ideal Intro Age: 24 Months
Age Range: 24 to 36 Months

This elegant homemade Blue Jeans Bag makes a young child feel very grown-up indeed.

Tools & Materials

- Pair of old blue jeans or other adult-sized pants with plenty of pockets and a button or snap closure

- Old cloth belt, or piece of fabric strap about 2″ wide and 24″ long

- Scissors

- Sewing machine or needle and thread

Directions

1. Cut both legs off the pants, about an inch below the crotch; put them aside for other projects.
2. Turn the remaining part of the pants inside out, sew closed the two leg openings, and turn right-side-out again.
3. To make the two tote bag handles:

   ○ Cut the belt or strap into two 12″ pieces.

   ○ Sew one end of each strap onto the inside of the front waistband; each should be attached about 4″ from the center closure point.

   ○ Sew the other end of each strap onto the inside back waistband, opposite the point where attached to the front.

HINTS

1. A sewing machine really simplifies this process. You *can* make it by hand, but it does take longer.
2. Save the legs; one can be used for making the Punching Bag, page 111. The other? Well, use your imagination.

Play Tips

○ Find the Toy: You hide a favorite small toy somewhere in this bag, then ask your toddler to find it. Well done!

○ Encourage your toddler to fill the pockets with smaller toys, stuffed animal friends, and the like.

○ Invent little stories you and your toddler can act out. One idea: Set an adult-sized chair beside a toddler-sized one. This makes a car in which you two can take a short trip. Make sure he packs everything you need.

○ Have a backyard picnic. Your toddler can bring the blanket and nonspillable snacks in his dazzling new bag.

○ Hang the bag over your toddler's bedpost at night. It's great for storing all kinds of otherwise unstorable toys. Plus a stuffed pal peeking out of the top can keep a protective eye on slumber.

Housekeeping Props

Even daily housekeeping chores seem romantic when you're a toddler; after all, he sees his beloved parents do them. Cut down the handles of an old broom and mop to toddler size. If he demands authenticity, and his wet mopping indoors is too messy, give him his junior mop and a pail of water and let him clean the porch or sidewalk.

Cut down the handles of an old broom and mop to make a toddler-sized housekeeping set.

Cars & Trucks

Toy vehicles of all kinds are favorites because they suit both action and fantasy play.

Toddlers love action. They revel in their new abilities to walk and run. They love to make things move, to pull and push and throw toys. They love to watch things move—a car, a truck, a plane, a dog or cat. Even favorite first words are the names of things that move: *car, ball, dog.* Toy vehicles certainly fit this interest.

Older toddlers also use toy vehicles in fantasy play. Real cars and trucks and planes, and the people who drive them, are big, exciting things to your toddler. When he acts out scenes with his toy counterparts, he's important, too.

Nearly any type of play vehicle is welcome. Small cars and trucks can also fit into your purse or pocket for play on outings. Make sure, though, that the wheels and other tiny pieces are firmly attached; should they come loose, your toddler might put them into his mouth. Larger vehicles offer more dramatic play on the floor. Start your collection now; it'll continue to grow throughout preschoolhood.

As of this writing, there are a few sturdy plastic trucks on the toy market that are specifically designed for toddlers. They're large and easy to push and have some special features:

- Removable parts that can be stacked and fitted onto the truck various ways; these serve as additional props in fantasy play.
- Cargo holds for storing things.
- Cargo hold covers or dump-trucklike dumpers that lift up easily.

Such trucks offer stacking/fitting play for the younger toddler, fantasy for the older, and action for both.

Supply some props with the vehicles, too. Small ones can fit into a shoebox garage (cut a few tunnel-shaped openings in one of the long sides), larger ones can be housed in a garage made from a cardboard box. Your toddler's indoor sliding board is a nice mountain for driving up and down. Or try this homemade Road Ramp 'n Tunnel.

ROAD RAMP 'N TUNNEL

Ideal Intro Age: 24 Months
Age Range: 24 to 36 Months

For highway adventures, make a Road Ramp 'n Tunnel.

Tools & Materials

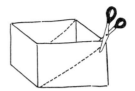

- Large cardboard box
- Yardstick
- Pencil
- Scissors or sharp knife
- Felt-tipped markers (optional)
- Strong tape (optional)

Directions

1. Cut off the top flaps.
2. Using the pencil and yardstick, draw a diagonal on both sides of the box, as shown.
3. Cut the box in two on the diagonals, and discard the scrap piece.
4. Turn the remaining piece upside down, and that's the ramp. Cut a tunnel-shaped opening in each supporting side. Cover the cut edges with tape if they're sharp. If you like, decorate the slope to resemble a road.

Fantasy Vehicles

Besides making believe with toy vehicles, your toddler likes to drive one himself. The ride-ons he pushed around on at 15 months become the cars and fire trucks and ice cream vans he now commandeers throughout your house and yard. See the suggestions on page 106 for tips on choosing appropriate ride-ons.

This homemade car, simple as it may seem compared to the manufactured mobiles you can buy, has been a favorite of many toddlers I know. Maybe it's because of the simplicity, maybe because the sides offer a protected, cozy feeling to the fantasy driver. Since the box cradles and protects, you can push your toddler around the carpeted floor in this toy as fast as you like—he can't fall off or out. The plans here include a steering wheel that turns. If you're pressed for time or materials, omit this and just decorate a box to resemble a car.

○

BOX CAR

Ideal Intro Age: 24 Months
Age Range: 18 to 36 Months

Tools & Materials

- ○ Cardboard box your child can sit in comfortably

- ○ 2 or 3 paper plates, the rigid molded type with a rim (Chinet)

- ○ large 2-pronged brass fastener

- ○ Large metal washer*

A cozy homemade Box Car inspires countless auto motive journeys.

*If you don't have a large metal washer, make one from plastic; cut a large disc from the top of a plastic coffee can lid and punch a small hole through the center.

○ Scissors or sharp knife

○ Felt-tipped markers

○ Tape

Directions

1. Cut three flaps off the top of the box, leaving one short flap (the steering wheel attaches to this).
2. Tape the paper plates together around their perimeter to make a steering wheel; the double or triple thickness adds durability.
3. Punch holes in the center of the paper plates and the flap.
4. Thread the washer onto the brass fastener; insert the fastener through the paper plates and the flap, flatten out the ends on the underside of the flap, and cover the ends with strong tape.
5. Decorate the remainder of the flap to resemble a dashboard (dials, etc.), and the outside of the box to resemble a car: doors on the sides, headlights and taillights, black half-circles on the bottom for wheels, and so on.

TO SUM UP

Can you remember all the way back—three years ago, is it?—when your child was just a tiny, probably wrinkly and squally newborn, dependent on you for almost everything? And now he's an independent almost-preschooler, with boundless skills and a storehouse of knowledge, ready to tackle new challenges. Amazing how much he's changed. And how much you've helped.

APPENDIXES

APPENDIX 1

Homemade Toys: Invaluable Materials

These are the standard items to keep on hand. They're listed alphabetically in case you want to refer back to this list when looking at a particular project.

Boxes
Boxes of all kinds and sizes are indispensable for making several of these projects. Get or save:

- Gift boxes, both the flat type that clothing usually comes in and the cubelike type.

- Shoeboxes, and like-sized boxes with lids.

- Mailing cartons, available fairly inexpensively at the post office. As of this writing, they come in three sizes, are sold flat so they're easy to transport, and are very sturdy when assembled.

- Larger cartons can be scrounged from liquor stores and other retail establishments. You can also buy excellent cartons, in many different sizes, from a moving company. Like the post-office cartons, they're sold flat and are very strong when assembled.

- For giant cartons, check with an appliance store. One mother I know chose several large cartons at a store, then paid to have them delivered to her home (just as she would have paid to have an appliance delivered).

Clothing, Towels, Linens
One of the easiest ways to make a stuffed toy or pillow is to use existing fabric objects rather than to cut out patterns from flat material. Socks, gloves, T-shirts, old

blue jeans, washcloths and hand towels, and pillowcases can all be transformed into wonderful items in a fraction of the time it would take to make them from scratch.

Elastic Strap
Elastic strap, about an inch wide, is terrific for hanging toys on the crib or stroller or gym, or just for dangling toys from your hand, because it stretches and gives when your baby pulls the object.

Fabric
All kinds, all patterns, all textures. If you haven't already, now's the time to start a scrap box. Look for odds and ends and remnants at fabric stores. Save old clothing and bed linens. Always prewash fabric that you think might shrink.

Glue
Regular white household glue (such as Elmer's). It's nontoxic, dries clear, and readily washes out should you spill some.

Markers
A good set of felt-tipped markers is a must. Choose the nontoxic washable type, in case your child should get into them.

Mat or Hobby Knife
Sometimes called a utility knife, this consists of a handle with a triangular, very sharp, replaceable blade. A *mat knife* comes in different sizes, from slender as a pencil to thick as a screwdriver handle. Unbeatable for cutting things out of cardboard.

Mylar
Metallized polyester film (popularly called Mylar) is a thick cellophanelike plastic that's durable, machine washable, dryer safe (at low heat), and noisy when handled. Use Mylar to stuff all or parts of fabric toys; when your baby squeezes the toy, he'll love the delightful crackly sound. Those helium-filled "mirrored" balloons are usually made of Mylar. Save them! You can also buy Mylar in some home decorating centers. It's sold by the yard, like fabric.

Newspaper
Great stuffing material for blocks made from cardboard boxes and grocery bags, and even for some fabric toys that won't be washed.

Pictures
Eye-catchers for the young baby, room decorations, books—these and other favorites are all made of pictures. Rather than saving tons of heavily illustrated magazines and catalogues, cut out pictures that might one day be useful and discard the rest of the magazine. Remember that young children love animals, so also look for nature magazines like *Smithsonian*, *National Geographic*, and *Ranger Rick*. Other sources of pictures:

- Old calendars.

- Posters, especially for room decorations.

- Reproductions of paintings from the art museum; these usually come in both postcard and small poster size.

- Picture postcards.

- Wrapping paper with bold, bright designs.

Sewing Machine
Not essential, but extremely handy. Some of the fabric toys will probably take longer than 30 minutes if you do them with needle and thread.

Stuffing
Polyester fiberfill (sometimes called spun polyester) is sold by the bag at sewing, fabric, and do-it-yourself stores. Get *lots;* you'll be surprised at how much stuffing you can cram into even a small fabric toy. Shredded foam stuffing is also good, but is heavier and takes longer to dry after washing. You can also stuff small toys with old nylons and pantyhose.

Tape
Handy to have different kinds:

○ Cellophane or "magic" tape (such as Scotch tape), for taping pictures into books, etc.

○ Masking tape, for taping pictures on walls, etc.

○ Wrapping or packing tape, such as used for wrapping up boxes for shipping. This tape sticks very securely and is very strong. Look for a roll about 2″ thick; it's available in stationery and office supply stores. NOTE: this is *not* masking tape; masking tape does not stick nearly as securely.

Yarn
Several projects call for thick, soft yarn. This is the very heavy yarn that's used for wrapping presents or tying up ponytails (still?), *not* yarn that's used for knitting. Like elastic strap, thick yarn is invaluable for hanging and displaying toys.

APPENDIX 2
Homemade Toys: By Materials and Techniques